D1442161

teenvirtue2

A TEEN GIRL'S GUIDE TO RELATIONSHIPS

teenVirtue2

A TEEN GIRL'S GUIDE TO RELATIONSHIPS

by vicki courtney

BROADMAN
&HOLMAN
PUBLISHERS

TEENVIRTUE:
REAL ISSUES, REAL LIFE.

TeenVirtue 2: A Teen Girl's Guide to Relationships
Copyright © 2006 by Vicki Courtney
All rights reserved.
Printed in the United States of America

Published by Broadman & Holman Publishers
Nashville, Tennessee

Ten-digit ISBN: 0-8054-4191-3
Thirteen-digit ISBN: 978-0-8054-4191-8

Dewey Decimal Classification: 305.23
Subject Heading: Domestic Relations\Teenagers\Adolescent Psychology

1 2 3 4 5 6 7 8 9 10   10 09 08 07 06

AUTHOR WEB SITES TO CHECK OUT

www.virtuousreality.com—features online magazine for preteen, teen, college, and adult women.

www.virtuousreality.com/events—provides a schedule of upcoming Yada Yada and Yada Yada Junior events for girls ages third through twelfth grades and mothers; also information about how you can bring an event to your area.

www.vickicourtney.com—to view Vicki Courtney's current speaking schedule or to find information about inviting her to speak.

www.virtuepledge.com—features an online community where girls and young women can pledge themselves to biblical virtue.

OTHER BOOKS BY VICKI COURTNEY FROM BROADMAN & HOLMAN PUBLISHERS

TeenVirtue: Real Issues, Real Life . . . A Teen Girl's Survival Guide

Your Boy: Raising a Godly Son in an Ungodly World

Your Girl: Raising a Godly Daughter in an Ungodly World

Yada Yada: A Devotional Journal for Moms

More Than Just Talk: A Journal for Girls

The Virtuous Woman: Shattering the Superwoman Myth

Table of Contents

Your Relationship with . . . Family

Your Relationship with . . . God

ABOUT THE AUTHORS

VICKI COURTNEY is the Founder of Virtuous Reality Ministries, which reaches over 150,000 girls and moms a year through events, an online magazine for teen girls, (www.virtuousreality.com), and resources. She is a national speaker and the best-selling author of *TeenVirtue: Real Issues, Real Life . . . A Teen Girl's Survival Guide.* She lives in Austin, Texas, with her husband, Keith, and three children, Ryan, Paige, and Hayden. To find out more, visit her Web site at www.vicki courtney.com.

SUSIE DAVIS communicates with girls and women of all ages, including Virtuous Reality sponsored Yada Yada events for teen girls and their mothers. In addition, she is the author of *The Time of Your Life: Finding God's Rest in Your Busy Schedule.* She lives in Austin, Texas, with her husband, Will, and three children, Will III, Emily, and Sara. To find out more, visit her website at www.susiedavisministries.com.

WHITNEY PROSPERI has a heart for girls and girls' ministry. She is the author of *Life Style: Real Perspectives from Radical Women in the Bible,* a twelve-week Bible study for middle and high school girls. Her newest offering, *Girls Ministry 101* will be published in August 2006 by Youth Specialties. She lives in Tyler, Texas, with her husband, Randy, daughter, Annabelle, and has a second child on the way.

A special thanks also goes to **JULIE SHANNAN** for contributing several quizzes.

INTRODUCTION

If I asked you to make a list of the things you treasure most in your life, what would be on your list? Definitely, your cell phone—I mean, who could live without that? What about your first place ribbon from the 3rd-grade science fair? Or maybe, an endearing love note or IM message from your crush? You are saving those, right? What about your favorite blankie or stuffed animal from when you were a baby? Or how about that shoe box of notes from your friends from your grammar school years? Maybe, the gold locket your dad gave you on your six-year birthday or your old Beanie Baby collection? How about your trophies or a clipping from the newspaper where your name was listed for making the honor roll?

I heard a speaker once say, "Relationships are the key to life." If that's true, then maybe our "list of treasures" should include the names of family members, friends, and most importantly, God. It's amazing when you think that you're required to go to school for thirteen years to learn about the three "r's," but you're pretty much on your own when it comes to the most important "r." And when it comes to a final grade, many people are flunking out in their relationships. What good is a high school diploma if you don't have the people skills to succeed in a job? What good are fame and fortune if you have no one to share it with? What good is a bunch of knowledge if one-half of the population can't even make a marriage work? Most importantly, when it comes to the relationship that matters most of all, Jesus said it best in Mark 8:36 when He asked, "For what does it benefit a man to gain the whole world yet lose his life?"

I would have to agree that "relationships are the key to life." And they are too important to risk failing. *TeenVirtue 2* was created to be a survival guide of sorts when it comes to the relationships that matter most in life—your relationships with friends, family, guys, and God. Each article includes "Can you relate?" questions at the end to get you thinking on a deeper level. You can answer the questions on your own, with a close friend, or in a group setting. Kind of like mini pop quizzes, but on a subject that's a little more exciting than reading, writing, or 'rithmetic. ☺

— Vicki Courtney

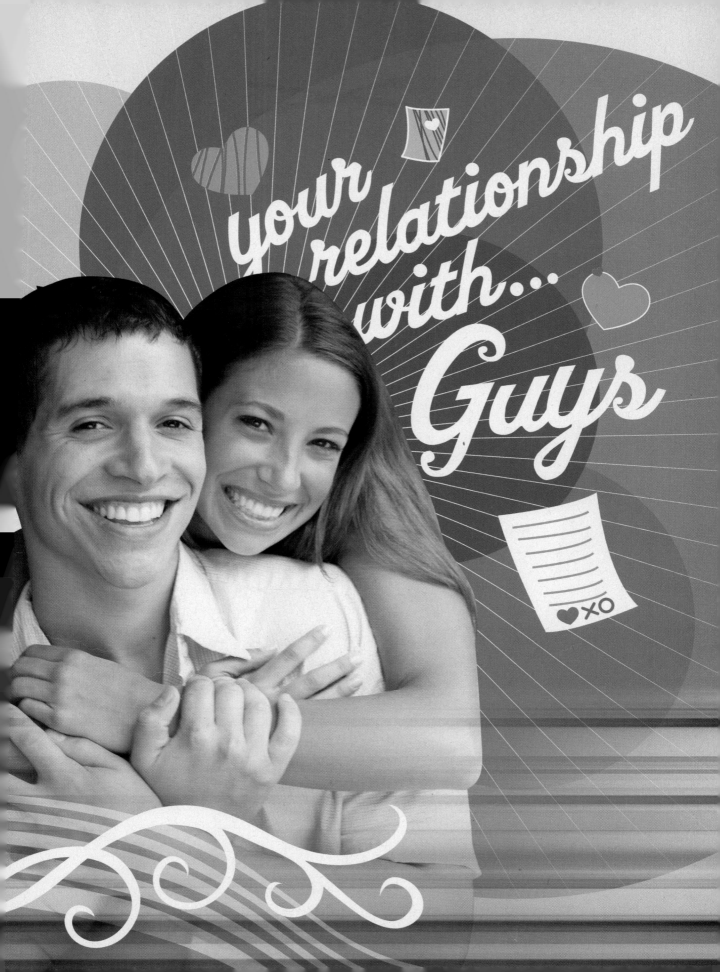

your relationship with... Guys

DO YOU ~~WANT~~ NEED A BOYFRIEND?

Meggy1234> Hey, you seemed like you were in a bad mood earlier at Amanda's. You OK?

justagirl> No, I'm sick of Caleb messing with my feelings.

Meggy1234> What do you mean?

justagirl> HE'LL TEXT ME FOR A WEEK STRAIGHT

justagirl> THEN STOP for no reason

justagirl> AND WE WONT TALK FOR awhile

justagirl> AND then Amanda said he had texted her yesterday

justagirl> AND IM SICK OF IT

justagirl> I DONT KNOW

justagirl> I DONT CARE

justagirl> I HAVE TO GET HIM OUT OF MY HEAD

Meggy1234> Yep, you have to get over him

justagirl> It's so hard! HE WAS MY FIRST! MY FIRST REAL BOYFRIEND, FIRST REAL KISS

justagirl> isn't that supposed to mean something?

Meggy1234> well yeah, but you guys broke up months ago

justagirl> Meg, you don't understand

justagirl> all I ever wanted was a boyfriend

justagirl> and then Caleb asked me out

justagirl> When we were together I FINALLY FELT LIKE I WAS WORTH SOMETHING

justagirl> AND THEN a month later he gave me the stupid let's be friends speech

justagirl> AND it left me feeling like a big NOTHING

Meggy1234> Ah, I'm sorry ☹

justagirl> I HAVE PEOPLE SURROUNDING ME, BUT I STILL FEEL SO EMPTY INSIDE

Meggy1234> yeah, that stinks

justagirl> LIKE I GO OUT WITH FRIENDS, BUT IM STILL LONELY, LIKE ON THE INSIDE

Meggy1234> having a boyfriend is not going to solve your problem

Meggy1234> I've told you that before

justagirl> I know I know but it would help, right?!

by Vicki Courtney

It's amazing how so many girls think that having a boyfriend will fill their hearts with that warm fuzzy feeling forever, as in "happily ever after" kind of forever. One too many bedtime fairy tales, I suppose. Sure, there's nothing like that in-love feeling, especially in the beginning of the relationship. Something about having a boyfriend makes you feel acceptable.

Out of a sea of anxious girls, someone actually noticed you, was attracted to you, and picked you. It validates that you are worth something to someone else other than your family and closest friends. You are someone's girlfriend. And you have a boyfriend.

I was definitely boy crazy when I was in school. My first official boyfriend (if you can call him that) came rather unexpectedly on the first day of fifth grade. A classmate sitting in the desk behind me tapped me on the shoulder and handed me a folded-up note. Before I mistakenly assumed that he was the sender, he quickly pointed to a cute boy with a shaggy haircut sitting a couple of desks behind him and whispered, "It's from him." I unfolded the note and read the following words: "I like you. Will you go with me? Circle YES or NO. From, Dorwin." I didn't know a thing about this boy except that he was rumored to hold the school record for the one-hundred-yard dash. Sounded like good credentials to me, so with little thought, I circled YES and passed the note back. I'm pretty sure my heart skipped a beat when I glanced back and saw him open the note and smile. We were officially "going steady." Yeah, I know it sounds kind of goofy, but that's what we called it back then. Sometimes guys would even give you a clunky silver ID bracelet with their name on it, a gesture that made it even more official. I was awarded the ID bracelet on the second day of school, and voilà, I had myself a boyfriend.

Not unlike the unspoken rules of today's elementary and middle school romances, it officially meant that we would hardly say two words to each other from that moment forward. We would, however, hold hands under the lunch table, as agreed upon in one of many notes we passed back and forth at the beginning of the year. The first time he grabbed my hand under that lunch table, I knew I was hooked. I think I had a perfect attendance record that year. In fact, I remember getting irritated at my mother for having the nerve to switch over midyear to fold-over lunch baggies because they had been on sale. Didn't she know how important it was for me to be able to single-handedly shake a sandwich out of its bag?! For one month I had to rip the sandwich baggie open with my teeth. So much for trying to impress this guy!

> **"YOU ARE TO NEVER BOW DOWN TO ANOTHER GOD BECAUSE THE LORD, BEING JEALOUS BY NATURE, IS A JEALOUS GOD."**

And thus began my string of boyfriends. Throughout middle school and high school, I almost always had a boyfriend. I never stopped to think that going from boyfriend to boyfriend might indicate a deeper problem. Like the girl in the IM a couple pages back, I had allowed a boyfriend to be the foundation of my worth. Having a boyfriend meant that I was desirable and worth something. Not having a boyfriend meant that I was not. Or so I thought. Funny thing though, even when I had a boyfriend, my heart never felt at peace. The initial flutter in my heart that came the beginning of the relationship always wore over time.

I understand wh being in a relationshi never quite did the tric Exodus 34:14 says, "Yo are to never bow dow to another god becaus the LORD, being jealou by nature, is a jeal ous God." When Go made this declara tion though Moses he was concerned about his people the Israelites, put ting a higher prior ity on other things and neglecting the one thing tha mattered—their relationship with him. Another

> **HAVING A BOY-FRIEND IN GOD'S WILL AND TIMING CAN BRING SATISFACTION, BUT IT WAS NEVER MEANT TO BRING WORTH.**

nslation says the verse this way: "You must worship no other gods, but only the LORD, for he is a God who is passionate about his relationship with you" (NLT). Isn't that incredible? God is *passionate about his relationship with you!* We were created to love him above all else; and until we do, our hearts will never be fully satisfied. Not by money, power, achievements, popularity, beauty, or having a boyfriend. Having a boyfriend in God's will and timing can bring *satisfaction,* but it was never meant to bring *worth.*

How I wish I had known this truth at your age! Fortunately, God stuck with me over the years. He was "jealous" to take his rightful place in my heart, a place that I had attempted to fill with a steady stream of boyfriends. Finally, at the age of twenty-one, I surrendered my heart to him and my life has never been the same. I was his and he was mine. I felt worth, value, and purpose in life. Who needs a silver ID bracelet when the God of this universe is waiting to inscribe his name upon your heart?✱

1. Have you been guilty of thinking a boyfriend could increase your worth? If yes, how do you feel about it, now?

2. How does it feel to know that God is "passionate about his relationship with you" and that he loves you with a "jealous" love?

3. What positive results might we see if more girls were aware of the above truth?

QUIZ: don't get Crushed

Have you ever had a crush on someone? Maybe the lifeguard at the pool, your brother's friend, or that cute new boy in algebra class? A little crush from time to time is perfectly normal, but if your crushing progresses from a little to a lot, it can be hazardous to your health. If you're not careful, constant crushing can consume your thought life and distract you from reality.

by Julie Shannan

The last thing you think about before you drift off to sleep is:

a) One little lamby, two little lambies, three little lambies, . . .

b) Romeo, Romeo, wherefore art thou Romeo?

You sign on instant messenger and see that your best friend and crush are both online. You:

a) IM your friend and ask about her day

b) Send your crush a flirty message and hope for a reply

It's football season, and you don't miss a game because:

a) It gives you a chance to hang out with all your friends

b) You might get a chance to sit next to your crush in the stands

Sunday night youth group just got better because:

a) Your group just started a new series you're really excited about

b) Your crush just started going to your church

You got your new locker assignment and you:

a) Check your schedule to see if it's close to your first-period class

b) Pray that it's within a ten-locker radius of your crush

Your friend invites you to movie night at her house, and you ask her:

a) What movie she's planning on showing?

b) Who she's inviting—if your crush is on the list, it's a "yes!"

Track is not really your sport, but you join the track team because:

a) They're really desperate for one more relay runner

b) Your crush is on the team, and you'll get to see him every weekend

Every Tuesday night you volunteer at the community center because:

a) You love working with the kids and making a difference

b) Your crush's basketball team plays on that night

u're in study hall, and you:

Hit the books so you don't have gobs of homework when you get home

Lay your head on your desk and day dream about your crush

's the weekend, and you try to find out what your:

Friends are up to so you can hang with them

Crush is doing so you can "accidentally" run into him

otal your number of b's to discover where your heart resides most of the time:

0–3: Real World—You might have a small crush, but your feet are firmly planted on solid ground. You value your friendships over your crush. Instead of making plans around your crush, you spend your days having a great time with your friends.

4–6: Out to Lunch—One minute your feet are on the ground, and the next minute your head is in the clouds. If you're not careful, your crushing may start to distract you from real world matters. Be sure to guard your thoughts and focus your attention on reality.

7–10: La-La Land—You are crushing so hard that you're missing out on all the fun. Learn to redirect your wandering thoughts every time you start thinking about your crush. Daydreaming about something you don't have will only bring you discontentment. Decide today that instead of wasting precious time wishing for what you don't have, you will start enjoying the things you do have. ✱

Life Lessons with Barbie and Ken

by Vicki Courtney

February 12, 2004, marked a sad day for Barbie lovers, young and old. Just two days before Valentine's Day, a press release was made stating that after forty-three blissful years as America's most famous plastic couple, Barbie and Ken were splitting up. Barbie's business manager (yes, you heard crisis. Maybe our first clue should have been when she got the pink Corvette. Or maybe the real reason behind this pre-manufactured publicity stunt was that Mattel wanted to sell more dolls and knew that in order to do so, they would have to mold Barbie to fit the anti-marriage, pro-hook-up culture of today. While I don't want to take the Barbie break-up charade too

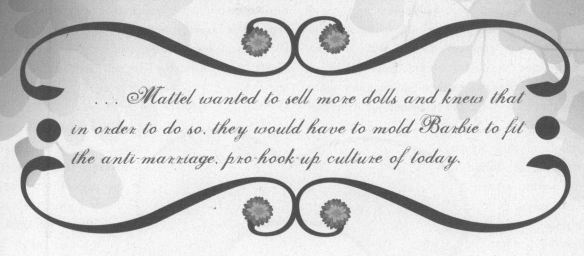

. . . Mattel wanted to sell more dolls and knew that in order to do so, they would have to mold Barbie to fit the anti-marriage, pro-hook-up culture of today.

me—she has a business manager) announced, "They feel it's time to spend quality time—apart," said Russell Arons, vice president of marketing for Mattel. Considering that three Barbie dolls are sold every second around the world, it must have come as a blow to many girls, who at some point, had marched their Barbies down a pretend aisle dressed in their lacy bridal gowns and veils to say their "I do's" to their beloved Kens. I can still recall to this day my best friend and I giggling at that magical moment when we would make Barbie and Ken kiss to seal the deal.

What is this world coming to when Barbie and Ken split? Barbie and Ken were supposed to be 2-gether 4-ever, period, end of sentence. By the end of the day, rumors were flying as to the real reason behind the couple's decision to take their relationship to Splitsville. One rumor had it that Barbie's career had gotten in the way. Let's face it; the woman has had more than ninety careers, including a run for the White House. That many career changes can definitely take a toll on a marriage. Another rumor had it that Barbie now has her eye on a younger, hipper, Aussie surfer dude named Blaine. Chalk it up to the standard fashion doll midlife

far, I do find it sad that the times are such that Mattel felt it would boost sales if Barbie wasn't tied down in a fuddy-duddy, boring, long-term relationship to the same guy. In order for Barbie to fit into the times, Mattel announced that she had to be "single and available."

When I was a little girl, my friends and I spent long hours preparing our Barbies for the ball that was to happen that evening. Every weekend was homecoming weekend in Barbieland. Barbie and her numerous clones would gather together at my best friend's Barbie mansion (I only had the pop-up camper) and spend the entire day getting ready for their dates. The troop of Kens would arrive on time in a convoy of sports cars and jeeps, walk to the door, ring the doorbell, and gasp on cue when our Barbies descended the staircase. They would escort our dolls to their cars and even open their car doors!

After an evening of dancing in the arms of our Kens (no grinding allowed—we didn't even know such a thing existed), our Barbies were escorted home, walked to the door; and some, but not all, received a light kiss on the cheek. Once inside, the slumber party began, and our Barbies stayed up giggling the night away over miniature fake popcorn and two-liter Cokes. It wasn't unusual for a wedding or two to follow the next day. After a proper proposal, we would all join in on a chorus of "dum, dum, da dum" as the lucky doll made her way down the aisle to meet her groom. It was just understood that someday, we were all waiting for a turn to walk down that aisle—not just in Barbieland but in real life.

Today's Barbies need not stock their closets of their Malibu beach houses or Barbie mansions with extravagant ball gowns, boas, and stilettos. Miniature hooker-ware is the fashion staple of the new, chic, and ever-so-trendy Barbies of today. Lucky for Ken and Blaine, they no longer have to go to the trouble of asking Barbie out on a real date. Barbie doesn't date anymore, and she sure doesn't sit around dreaming about such silly things as marriage. My critics would say, "Look, Barbie and Ken grew apart. Barbie woke up one morning, like countless other women, and realized that she and Ken had absolutely nothing in common anymore. They had simply grown out of love." I can certainly understand that. In fact, I never really thought Barbie and Ken were much of a match in the first place. Coming from Texas, I always thought Ken was a little too mamby-pamby metro for my taste. Now, that GI Joe—he was a real man. But, for whatever reasons, Barbie had chosen Ken to be her lifelong love. It was her storybook romance, not mine.

In the end Barbie, like countless others, defined love as a feeling, rather than a commitment. Not that they hadn't survived their share of tough times. They stuck it out through her numerous career changes including military medic in Desert Storm, an astronaut, a paleontologist, an Olympic athlete, a fashion model, and a rock star. Ken endured Barbie's forty-three pets, including twenty-o dogs, twelve horses, three ponies, six cats, a parrot, a chimpanzee, a panda, a lion cub, a giraffe, and a zebra. They ev survived the countless questions that emerged over the yea about Ken's sexuality. When it was all said and done, the wonder couple would join the ranks of the rest of the "wond couples" of the world: the J-Los and Bennifers, the Brad an Jennifers. When the going got tough, the couple would ju split because that's what couples do today.

I can't help but wonder if gir today, deep down inside, woul choose to return to the sim pler days of innocence an purity if given the oppor tunity. You know, the days when girl dreamed about meeting that one special guy who would sweep them off their feet, ask them out on dates, pay their way, court them, woo them, and eventually, get on one knee and propose with a ring and a dozen roses. Ah, but who am I fooling? Such dreams are silly when you can instead, hook up for the night with no strings attached and then move on to another Ken or Blaine. Next thing you know, Mattel will introduce Party Barbie with an optional fold-up neighborhood pub to set the stage for her future boy toy pickups. I wouldn't be surprised to find it stocked with miniature dartboards, frosted mugs of beer, and a condom dispenser in the bathroom. By then, Surfer Blaine will have changed into Bartender Blaine and Party Barbie and Hookup Midge, dressed in their midriff-baring tight tees and micro minis, will have their eyes on other boys at the bar.

We must catch up with the times, and the times have declared that "happily ever after" is about living for the moment and, above all, living for self. Funny, but the hookup culture never highlights the moments after a hookup has occurred. They never talk about the emptiness that

And I pray that you, being rooted and established in love, may have power, together with all the saints, to grasp how wide and long and high and deep is the love of Christ, and to know this love that surpasses knowledge—that you may be filled to the measure of all the fullness of God. (Ephesians 3:17b–19 NIV)

ost girls feel after exercising their "sexual freedom." They ever talk about the "walk of shame," common on many rge college campuses. Girls who casually hookup can be und walking back to their dorms, alone, in the middle of e night—heads down, not wanting to be recognized. One n only imagine what they are thinking on their long walk me. I bet a good many of them would give anything to go ack to their more innocent days of playing Barbie. Back to the days when Barbie's biggest worry was over what to wear to the ball—not what to wear, or do, to get Ken or Blaine to look her way, pursue her, and ~~love~~ use her. If you ask me, that's one warped version of "happily ever after." In fact, it makes me want to head up to the attic, brush the dust off my fifteen-year-old daughter's trunk of Barbies, and beg her to play just one more time. ✱

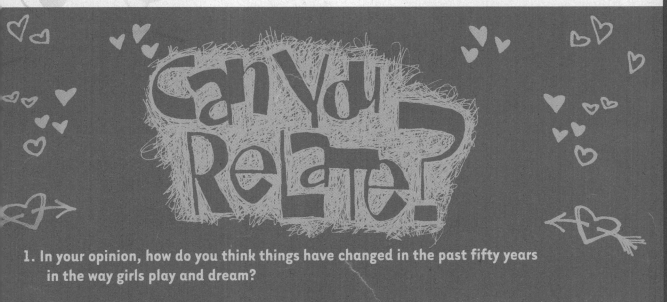

Can You Relate?

1. In your opinion, how do you think things have changed in the past fifty years in the way girls play and dream?

2. What sort of larger message does Barbie's newfound single status send to girls today?

3. Describe some of the ways you played and dreamed when you were little.

4. Do you ever wish you were little again? Why or why not?

5. Do you think hooking-up will produce the happiness girls long for?

6. "Happily ever after" can only be found by entering into a long-term relationship with _____. (Hint: The answer is not Ken!)

the "nice guys' list

by Vicki Courtney

Nice guys are not born; they are made. Back when I was ministering to college women, I was disturbed at the number young ladies who would tell me that "nice Christian guys" are rare on their campuses and in their church groups. They shar that the Christian guys were no different from the rest of the guys out there when it came to rude behaviors, sexual joke immaturity, and lack of respect for women. How sad! Christians are called to be set apart from the world. That being sa our Christian guys should be held to a higher standard when it comes to the way they interact with girls or how they beha in dating relationships. Below, you will find the nice guys' checklist. Some of these may seem out of date or old-fashione but you deserve the very best—God's best!

nice guys . . .

never discuss details of a dating relationship with their frien or anyone for that matter. It will almost always come back haunt them.

stay true to their friends. If they are considering asking out a friend of a past girlfriend or a buddy's past girlfriend, they will wait a suitable amount of time and, if need be, give the friend or past girlfriend the heads-up beforehand.

never ask a girl out over IM, text-message, or through e-mail. Period, end of sentence.

do not build a relationship with a girlfriend solely by means of IM and text messaging. Some conversations were meant to occur by phone call or face-to-face.

are not in the habit of belching, passing gas, swearing, and other abominable behaviors in front of the opposite sex. Girls should be treated like girls—not like "one of the guys."

do not believe in "going Dutch" when they have a girlfriend. Some exceptions might be made (expensive concerts, etc.), but they should be the exceptions, not the rule.

never flirt with someone else's girlfriend. There will be many insecure girls who initiate the flirting to bait for the attention they crave, but most guys see through this behavior and recognize that they are one of many boys being flirted with.

never ever engage in sexual banter with the opposite sex. Insecure girls may laugh along with them, but deep down inside they feel disrespected and devalued.

recognize the importance of prayer for making wise choices and avoiding temptations in a relationship.

never expect the girl they are dating to set the physical limits in the relationship. They have determined their own limits according to God, up front.

behave nobly after the breakup. They do not vent their hurt or anger publicly or seek revenge.

flee tempting situations. No need to explain. If need be, they run for their lives and explain later.

never end relationships over the telephone or by IM, e-mail, or text messaging. Further, they do not ask friends to deliver the bad news. If she was important enough to ask out in the first place, she is important enough to end the relationship in person.

will not engage in physical intimacies (hand-holding, kissing, etc.) with girls they are not going out with.

treat past girlfriends with honor and respect. They do not betray them by sharing personal information with others.

make every effort to introduce themselves to the parents of the girl they are dating. With confidence and assurance, they know how to give a firm handshake to the girl's dad, make proper eye contact with him and the girl's mom, use proper manners ("Yes Sir," "No Ma'am"), be responsive to any questions they ask, and initiate conversation with them from time to time.

open car doors and other doors, allow their girl-friends to pass through doors ahead of them, as well as display other common acts of courtesy.

when *good Girls* LIKE BAD BOYS

by Susie Davis

AT SIXTEEN I MADE UP MY MIND. I JUST HAD TO HAVE A DATE WITH JEFF. HE WAS GORGEOUS . . . AND DANGEROUS. I KNEW JEFF HAD A "BAD BOY" REPUTATION. And I knew all the negative stuff I heard about him was likely true, but I had an obsession with getting a date with him. In my teenage mind he was just unbelievable. As a sophomore, he was quarterback of the varsity football team. He was also sought after by tons of girls at our high school. He was great to look at and as charming as ever. Forget the fact that I was a Christian girl trying to hold on to a good reputation. Forget the fact that my friends warned me that Jeff was not my type. Forget the fact that my youth minister always warned me, "Never date a guy you wouldn't marry." I wanted to go out with Jeff.

It took months before I got exactly what I wanted—a date with Jeff. He finally asked me out, and I have to tell you—it was one of the worst dates of my life. He was after one thing that I wasn't willing to give, so it made the evening rather uncomfortable. Let's just put it this way—he brought me home from the date early. Real early.

So I have a question for you that has been nagging me for years. Why are "good girls" attracted to "bad boys"? Is it the challenge? Is it about hoping to "fix" them? Is it about popularity? How can you explain the magnetic pull, the endless attraction that good girls have for bad boys? While we could debate the reasoning endlessly in an attempt to explain, one thing is sure: it is a dangerous idea to date a "bad boy."

Why? Because it is dangerous to entrust yourself to a guy that you know does not value what you value. For example, let's

say you are a virgin, and that is a value in your life based on the guidelines God has about sex outside of marriage. (The Bible says there shouldn't be any sex outside of marriage.) If your bad boy is sexually active and everyone knows it, don't fool yourself into thinking you are going to save him and redirect his values about sexual activity. If you date a loose guy, you might just end up losing everything you have worked so hard to save.

If you don't party but your bad boy drinks and does drugs, don't fool yourself into thinking you are going to be the one to pull him out of that dark hole. Besides, there are programs for people with problems like that.

If popularity is your thing and if you are hoping you will get some attention from dating guys like that, well, I have some news. You will. You'll get lots of attention from other guys just like the bad boy you are choosing to date.

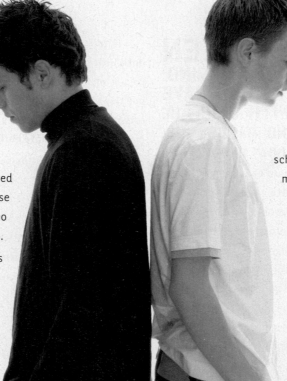

So while I don't know all the reasons nice girls are attracted to not-so-nice guys, I can promise a ton of heartache for girls who insist on going out with bad boys.

First Corinthians 15:33 has a promise that is very clear. "Do not be deceived: 'Bad company corrupts good morals.'"

If you make the choice to date and hang out with "bad company," then you can count on that corrupting your morals. Date a guy without high moral standards, and you could find yourself losing your high moral standards.

The reverse is also true. Why not start looking at the guys with good morals? Take what my youth minister said to heart and determine you'll never date a guy you wouldn't marry.

If you date in high school, keep in mind that every guy you date is a potential mate. That guy you are just dying to go out with could well become your husband. You might be thinking *Oh, come on. I'm just having fun dating these guys at my school. It's not that big of a deal if I go out with guys I know I would never marry. I'm just in high school. Dating doesn't have to be that serious.*

Although I can remember having the same kind of mentality, my life is a case in point. I married the guy I started dating when I was a sophomore in high school. It can happen. Fortunately for me, God really pounded in the importance of the principle of only dating marriage material, so thankfully, my bad-boy attraction and dating were limited. I managed to marry a good guy with good morals who loves God.

And while dating in high school may seem more like fun and games than serious business, you need to know you can fall in ve with a bad boy if you insist on dating one. Or you can ecide now that you won't go out with guys that don't have e same types of standards you have. And if you aren't xactly sure if the guy you'd like to date is up to your standards, think of him and ask yourself, "Is this the man I would ke to spend the next sixty something years of my life with?" nat's always a sobering question.

While the bad boy/good irl scene might make good rama (I love watching Rory igure out what to do with ess on reruns of *Gilmore Girls*), in real life it's dangerous business. Don't be fooled nto thinking you are strong enough to withstand the corruption that comes with bad company. It just won't work. And you are not the stand-alone exception to the 1 Corinthians promise. But the good news is you are able to stand alone and hold out for God's best for your life. God can strengthen you to reach his best in your life, even in your dating world.★

DON'T BE FOOLED INTO THINKING YOU ARE STRONG ENOUGH TO WITHSTAND THE CORRUPTION THAT COMES WITH BAD COMPANY.

Can You Relate?

1. What do you think causes 'good girls' to desire 'bad boys'?

2. "Bad company corrupts good morals." Can you think of a time when this principle was proven true in your life?

3. How might you protect yourself from allowing others to corrupt your morals?

4. What kind of guidelines do you have for dating? If you don't have any, consider making a short list of qualities you are looking for in a guy.

5. After making the list, use it as a standard in deciding whether you will accept a date with a guy in the future.

6. Think of a Christian friend you could ask to hold you accountable in the area of dating. Call her and ask for her help if you start to feel pulled in by the bad-boy magnetism.

The Girl in the

Pink Bikini

by Vicki Courtney

during my junior year of college, I lived in a condominium complex that was filled entirely with college students. It was only a year old and considered the "in place" to live. It had gated security, underground parking, and even a glass elevator!

Best of all, it had a pool and hot tub right smack in the middle of the complex, and every unit looked out onto the pool and courtyard. Once class was over (noon, for me—are you jealous?), if the sun was shining, you could pretty much bet that my roommate and I, not to mention just about every other girl who lived in the complex, would be by the pool (uh, studying, of course). Since the pool was located right in the middle of the complex and next to the elevator, we were used to catcalls from the guys passing by. Some would even call down from their balconies to get our attention. It was like a pool party every day.

One day, some guys (very cute ones, I might add) in the corner unit downstairs started talking to some girls by the pool and asked one of them to deliver a message to "the girl in the pink bikini," which happened to be me. The girl said they wanted to invite my roommate and me to a party they were having that night. We talked it over, yelled over a "maybe," and went back to more important matters—like working on our tans.

Later that night, we decided to stop by their party and check it out before heading out to meet friends. We knocked on the door, and a guy answered and yelled back

> ❝ Not only is it a sign of true friendship to confront a friend who is making sinful choices, it is scriptural. ❞

to his friends, "She's here! The girl in the pink bikini!" My roommate mumbled an "Oh, brother" under her breath. The guy who had answered the door literally did a body scan from head to toe and said, "You are our favorite girl to look at by the pool. The guys are going to be happy you're here." At the time I remember feeling somewhat uncomfortable by his remark, but at the same time I was also flattered.

My roommate and I stayed at the party for a little while and then headed out to meet other friends. But from that day forward, hidden in my heart was the fact that I had been singled out by a bunch of guys for having a "hot body." It made me feel so good that it became my incentive to stay in shape in the years to come. If I gained weight, I tortured myself by replaying that scene by the pool in my mind over and over again. It became my driving force to lose weight. My erratic pattern of yo-yo dieting and compulsive exercising eventually led to an eating disorder and low self-esteem.

Now, as I look back on the situation some twenty years later, I am appalled that I didn't understand what was really going on that day by the pool. Why didn't I recognize the shallowness of a bunch of guys liking a girl just for her body and nothing more? Do you think they cared if I was smart, or kind, or had a great personality? No way! To them I was nothing more than an object for their

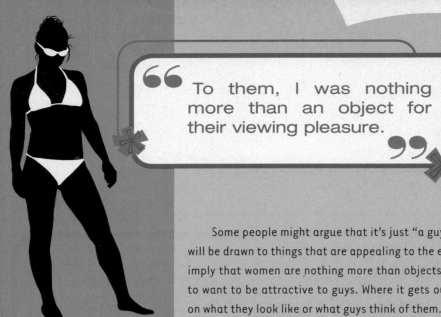

> ❝ To them, I was nothing more than an object for their viewing pleasure. ❞

viewing pleasure. I was not [a] person worth getting to kno[w]. In fact, can you believe th[at] not one of those guys eve[r] asked me my name at th[e] party? It didn't even matt[er] that I had a name. To the[m] I was "the girl in the pin[k] bikini." That's all. How cou[ld] I have ever been flattered[?] What a bunch of losers!

Some people might argue that it's just "a guy thing." Sure, guys are wired physically an[d] will be drawn to things that are appealing to the eye, but that does not excuse behaviors tha[t] imply that women are nothing more than objects. On the same note, it is not wrong for girl[s] to want to be attractive to guys. Where it gets out of balance is when girls base their wort[h] on what they look like or what guys think of them. Girls who do set themselves up for disaste[r] in the years to come. What do you think happens when the aging process kicks in a couple o[f] decades later? Eyebrows might raise if they show up at the pool in a pink bikini, but it won'[t] be because of their post-childbearing six-pack abs!

I am so grateful to finally know where true worth is found. Today I don't need to be noticed by others to feel good about myself. Psalm 139:17–18 reminds me that God's thoughts about me outnumber the grains of sand on the shore. With that knowledge my heart is at peace. I am loved by the one who matters most. I don't need a pink bikini to catch his eye. He loves me the same yesterday, today, and tomorrow—even twenty years more from now when I'm playing Marco Polo in the pool with my grandchildren. I'll probably be wearing one of those skirted one-pieces that I swore I'd never buy. Regardless, one thing is for certain: **I'll be precious in his sight.** ✶

Can You Relate?

1. Can you think of a time when a guy has given you attention for how you looked? If yes, how did it make you feel?

2. Would you ever date a guy who is more attracted to what you look like than who you are?

3. Do you feel good about yourself apart from attention you might receive from guys?

10 Never Evers

1. **Never ever** go into a guy's bedroom when his parents aren't home.

2. **Never ever** expect that you can make a decision about how far is too far in the heat of the moment.

3. **Never ever** entrust your heart to a guy who doesn't care about God.

4. **Never ever** go on a date with a guy who is drinking or doing drugs.

5. **Never ever** entangle yourself with a guy who has a hot temper.

6. **Never ever** think that you can understand everything a guy is thinking.

7. **Never ever** expect a guy friend to act like a girlfriend.

8. **Never ever** let a guy you don't know drive you in his car alone.

9. **Never ever** fool yourself into thinking you can give your body to a guy with the intention of gaining his love.

10. **Never ever** give your body (or even pieces of your body) to a guy outside of marriage.

A thing or two you need to know about GUYS

by Susie Davis

I am a guy advocate. An advocate is one that pleads the cause of another. So in this case, I am here to plead the case for guys because, frankly, I love guys. (I love guys so much that I ended up dating a really fabulous one and married him.) And because I love guys (mine in particular), I have made a point to study them and attempt to understand them. As a result of observing, reading up, and talking with other married friends, I have learned some things about how they think and what they're like. And I have the lucky assignment to share this wonderful information with girls like you. Because the truth is that you are probably curious about guys. You likely wonder why they act the way they do and what motivates them. You are probably interested in trying to attract them (at least the ones you like) and would give just about anything to understand them. I want to reassure you that all the feelings and questions you have

A girl should not miss the fact that testosterone will impact a guy in thought and deed for the rest of his life. I would say that is one of the most important things girls need to know about guys because this hormone is what causes a guy to think about and enjoy looking at a girl.

Basically, at about seventeen, a guy will have a maximum load of testosterone, which will mean that he could experience what I call the "sight/flight" phenomenon. The "sight/flight" phenomenon works something like this. Let's say a guy is in your math class busy working away at a problem. Then he looks up just in time to see his sixteen-year-old female classmate walk into the room. She just happens to have a drop-dead gorgeous body with little covering it. At this point, physiologically, the guy catches sight of her body, and the testosterone kicks in causing his original thought pattern to take flight. Instead of thinking about the math problem, he is consumed with the tantalizing body walking past him.

That is the way it works with testosterone. Now, what a guy does with the thought after that says a lot about his spiritual condition and his mental habits. If he is mature in Christ and wants to honor God in his mind, he will redirect his thoughts immediately and discontinue looking. But if he has no such spiritual reservoir, he will let his mind wander where these hormones lead him. Now before you rail at this guy and call him a pervert, I want you to know that it is extremely difficult for guys to turn off the hormonal urges once they get turned on. And

> The impact of testosterone will have many other profound influences on a boy's developing mind and body. In fact, it will affect his every thought and deed for the rest of his life.

are completely normal. It is the way God designed women, to be interested in men and vice versa.

The number one thing you need to know about guys is that they are really different from girls physically (I know you're probably thinking, *Duh. Oh really. Gosh, I never noticed.*) which affects their physiology. Now, while I am not going to get into all the differences physically between boys and girls, you might be interested to know what the main hormone responsible for those differences is: testosterone. You can say it out loud. It's not a dirty word and it is very important for you to understand. This hormone is responsible for maleness. Muscle development. Hairy arms and legs. Voice deepening. You get it. But there is something else you should know about this hormone. It is summed up well in this quote: "The impact of testosterone will have many other profound influences on a boy's developing mind and body. In fact, it will affect his every thought and deed for the rest of his life."[1]

the reason is, that is how God made them. God made guys with hormones that, in effect, create a desire to look at a woman's body. That does not make all guys perverts. In fact, a bunch of Christian guys exercise unbelievable control in their thought life and in their actions.

Instead of berating all those guys for acting like guys, what I'd really like for you to do is look around at your high school, notice how some of the girls are dressed, and remember what testosterone does. We cannot begin to imagine how many guys are experiencing the "sight/flight" phenomenon on a daily basis right there in the halls at school.

Think of it this way. Imagine that you love chocolate (not a stretch for many of us). But also imagine that as much as you love chocolate, you decided that you are not going to eat it. Well, let's say

> "Also, the women are to dress themselves in modest clothing, with decency and good sense; not with elaborate hairstyles, gold, pearls, or expensive apparel, but with good works, as is proper for women who affirm that they worship God."
>
> 1 Timothy 2:9–10

that you come to school with no breakfast in your stomach, and you walk into your math class. Now, just as you start to work on those stupid math problems (your stomach grumbling), in walks a guy with a chocolate bar. Not only that, he sits at the desk next to you and tears off a part of the wrapper, exposing the chocolate. OK, not only are you starving and craving the chocolate, but now you also must sit next to it, where you can see it and smell it. And let's say that you had to sit there the entire math class with that candy bar well within reach and concentrate on math. It would be pretty frustrating, wouldn't it?

The difference here, with my analogy, is that you and I don't have a chemical release in our body that triggers a love and craving of chocolate . . . though I'd love to blame my chocolate addiction on some brain chemistry. And guys do have a chemical in their bodies that triggers an interest and urge regarding sexual desire—testosterone.

So please note that when you decide to dress in a way that shows a lot of skin or that super girly form (and yes, your body is girly enough to get a guy's attention), you are enticing a guy to look, and your body acts as a trigger to their physiological response. That's just the way it is.

Look, I'm not asking you never to enjoy wearing a tank top (though you might want to throw a blouse on over it if it is especially low cut) or a cute skirt, but I am asking, as guy advocate, to think about how your clothing choice affects those guys in your life. The Christian guys, who are likely trying hard to keep their minds focused in the right direction, and the non-Christian guys who might not have any reason at all to turn away from staring at your body, possibly objectifying you. (Objectification is another way of saying a guy sees your body without really seeing you.) And while we cannot control how a guy will handle what he sees with his eyes, we as women have the ability to control how we cover and dress our bodies.

In 1 Timothy 2:9–10, Paul exhorts women to concentrate on modesty and decency. "Also, the women are to dress themselves in modest clothing, with decency and good sense; not with elaborate hairstyles, gold, pearls, or expensive apparel, but with good works, as is proper for women who affirm that they worship God." That's good advice, but is it where you live? Maybe my updated version of 1 Timothy 2:9–10 will make better sense for your world. "I want you girls to dress modestly, not with your boobs hanging out of your shirt, your T-shirt suffocating your rib cage, or your pants cut so low that your rear cleavage is exposed to the world. Don't flat iron your hair into oblivion, and watch out for too much makeup; but rather be pure and kind and passionate about Jesus first, thinking of him as you dress because he is the one you profess to worship, adore, and think of as first in your life."

Make your body match your heart. ✱

---

1. James Dobson, *Bringing Up Boys* (Wheaton, Ill.: Tyndale House, 2001), 20.

1. Now that you know a thing or two about the guys in your life, would you consider giving them a much-needed break by dressing modestly? How can you make that goal a reality in your life?

2. As you have come to realize that God made guys to respond through their eyes, how does that make you feel about the way guys look at you? Is there a chance that you enjoy having a guy stare at you too long?

3. How might you become accountable to a friend regarding your clothing choices?

4. Would you consider going through your closet with someone you respect spiritually and have a "What Not to Wear" for the benefit of the guys in your life?

5. Think and pray about committing to this statement which is part of the Virtue Pledge on www.virtuousreality.com (a Web site for Virtuous Reality Ministries):

"I realize the clothes I wear are a reflection of my heart and my intentions. I will not wear clothes of a revealing nature that may cause my Christian brothers to stumble spiritually. I will base my clothing choices on this question: 'If Jesus were to return today, would I feel comfortable coming face-to-face with him wearing this outfit?'"

WHAT GUYS REALLY THINK ABOUT

PUSHY GIRLS

by Vicki Courtney

I collect vintage magazines such as *Ladies Home Journal* and *Seventeen*. While recently thumbing through an edition of the *Journal* from 1950, I stumbled upon an advice column for high school girls. One submission made me laugh out loud, but amazingly, the advice given was timely for today. This is what it said: "Some days the boy I like is extra sweet to me and the next day he just flips me a casual 'hello' that he would flip to any girl. I had a wienie roast the other night and I invited him. **(I kid you not—it says that!)** He sort of played up to me all night. I have tried to make him jealous, but he says he doesn't care if I go with other boys. I often go to the drugstore where he works to see him, but he never calls me for a date."

Here is the advice given: "And just when would the boy have time to call you when you are chasing him all the time? Too much attention, too many invitations, and the unhappy habit of hanging around the place a boy works are the fastest ways to convince him that he sees enough of you without having you around as a date-mate too. Give him a chance to miss you once in a while!"

Times have certainly changed. No more waiting by the phone for that special boy to call. Nowadays, if a girl wants to talk to a boy, she sends him a quick IM or text message and waits for his response. A guy hardly thinks twice if a girl contacts him first. Just recently, my seventeen-year-old son was IMing back and forth with a girl he knows; and before they ended their conversation, she informed him that she doesn't normally IM a guy first. It was her way of letting him know that if he was interested in talking to her, he better initiate the conversation. My son was blown away by this as he was accustomed to most girls IMing, texting, and calling him first. After he finished his conversation with her, he IMed his sister (who was on the upstairs computer) to tell her about it. He has given

...ne permission to share the actual IM conversation he ...had with his sister:

> **ryan****>** so she ims me and we talk for a while
>
> **ryan****>** and then at end she said she was goin and wanted me to know she doesnt usually im guys first
>
> **paige****>** so?
>
> **ryan****>** and i thought that was pretty cool
>
> **paige****>** ohhh
>
> **paige****>** so do you like her or what are you trying to tell me out of this
>
> **ryan****>** naw im just sayin thats weird
>
> **ryan****>** and different
>
> **ryan****>** but kinda cool

Times have certainly changed. Fifty plus years later, the same fashion magazines, that were once doling out advice on how girls should avoid being overly aggressive and pushy with guys, are now advising girls to take charge and make the first move. I am certainly not saying that we need to retreat to past days where girls didn't speak unless spoken to, but it would be nice to find a balance. I have encouraged my own fifteen-year-old daughter to impose a similar standard and not make a habit of always initiating conversations with guys she may be interested in. There is no harm in asking a guy about a homework assignment or initiating conversations with her "guy friends," but when it comes to the guys who make her heart beat faster, let them do the pursuing. Trust me, if they are interested, they will do it.

The irony is that deep down inside, most girls want to be chased and pursued. They don't realize that by initiating conversations by IM, texting, or calling, they let the guys off the hook when it comes to the pursuit. As a mother of a teenage boy, I have witnessed this phenomenon up close. My seventeen-year-old son has never really had to "pursue" a girl because he is accustomed to them pursuing him first. No wonder he was so taken aback, as was evident in the IM to his sister, by a girl who refuses to IM, text, or

DEEP DOWN INSIDE, MOST GIRLS WANT TO BE CHASED AND PURSUED.

call him first. I'm sure it must be difficult when this young lady logs onto Instant Messenger and sees a sea of guys online that she would love to talk to and get to know. I'm sure she knows that these guys

have plenty of girls who IM them the minute they get online. And I'm sure it must be tempting at times to relax her standard and just join the crowd. How does she stand a chance unless she makes the first move? What is her reward in waiting? How about this for a reward: Guys who are interested in getting to know her, pursue her. She is one of few girls my son has gone to the trouble to initiate conversation with and, get this, ask out on an official date. The girls who contact him first with invitations to do this

> YOU ARE WORTH BEING PURSUED. YOU ARE WORTH BEING CHASED. YOU ARE WORTH BEING ASKED OUT ON A REAL, LIVE DATE. YOU ARE WORTH BEING TREATED LIKE A LADY.

and that don't require pursuit. And they don't require him to ask them out, pick them up, and pay their way.

It certainly makes you wonder if the advice given to the high school girl who wrote in to the 1950 *Ladies Home Journal* isn't still relevant for today. It bears repeating: "Too much attention, too many invitations and the unhappy habit of hanging around the place a boy works are the fastest ways to convince him that he sees enough of you without having you around as a date-mate too. Give him a chance to miss you once in a while!"

You are worth being pursued. You are worth being chased. You are worth being asked out on a real, live date. You are worth being treated like a lady. But first, you must act like a lady. If you set your standards high, you may not log as many IM, text, or phone conversations with guys as some of the other girls do, but you will narrow it down to the ones who think you're worth pursuing. I realize that waiting for the guy you like to initiate conversation is a radical concept in a culture that tells girls to make the first move. Why follow the crowd when you can be "weird, and different, but kinda cool"? ✳

1. Do you think the advice given in the 1950 *Ladies Home Journal* is still relevant today? If yes, in what ways?

2. What are the advantages to having a standard in place where you don't initiate conversations with guys you may be interested in?

3. Would you ever consider adopting such a standard? Why or why not?

4. Do you think you are worth being pursued?

FOR IN THIS HOPE WE WERE SAVED. BUT HOPE THAT IS SEEN IS NO HOPE AT ALL. WHO HOPES FOR WHAT HE ALREADY HAS? BUT IF WE HOPE FOR WHAT WE DO NOT YET HAVE, WE WAIT FOR IT PATIENTLY.

(ROMANS 8:24–25 NIV)

by Julie Shannon and Vicki Courtney

How Well do You Play

You are dying to get the cute guy's attention who sits behind you in geometry so you:

a) Accidentally drop your pencil to see if he'll pick it up for you.

b) Offer to be his tutor after he gets his test back and you hear him let out a grumble. Who cares if you're barely passing yourself?

c) Smile at him but don't break a sweat trying to get him to notice you.

You finish your homework early so you decide to get online and IM. You:

a) Do a quick scan to see if your crush is online. If he is, you IM him first.

b) Know the drill. You click on every cutie's name and send him your standard salutation: "Hey, lover."

Now you sit back and wait for replies. The game is on.

c) IM your friends and see how their day went.

The new guy in school is the most gorgeous guy you've seen walk through your school doors. All the girls are dying to meet him, and his locker is right next to your best friend's. You:

a) Consider telling your friend that your locker is jammed and asking to share hers for a few days.

b) Show up at your friend's locker dressed to kill, introduce yourself to him, ask to see his cell phone, and conveniently program your number in while telling him, "If you need anything, give me a call." Smile, flip hair, and walk off. Mission accomplished.

c) What? He has a locker beside your best friend's? Oh well, only time will tell if he's as gorgeous on the inside as he is on the outside. Everyone knows that matters more, right?

one week before homecoming, and you still don't have a date. You've already bought a dress so you:

Enlist your best friend to hint to a few guys that you're available.

Turn on the charm, baby. It's time for "operation ask-every-available-cute-guy-in-sight-who-is-breathing-until-one-says-yes."

Make plans to go with your unattached friends.

You and your buds meet at the movies on Friday night, and you really want to sit next to your crush so you:

a) Buy a large popcorn so you can offer to share it with him.

b) Forget the popcorn! While your friends are in line, you sprint into the theater and shimmy your way into the seat next to him. Friends? What friends?

c) Remind yourself that if he's interested in you he will make the effort to sit next to you or get in contact with you after the movie.

You have been called a flirt:

a) Once or twice. No harm in having a little fun, right?

b) Often. But hey, they're just jealous.

c) Never. It's just not who you are.

the Flirting Game?

FLIRT-O-METER

Flirting is a game, and some girls play it all too well. Remember that hammer game in the arcades at amusement parks? The one where you hit the target to see if you can ding the bell at the top? How would your flirting abilities measure in the game?

MOSTLY BS: HIGH—Ding, ding, ding! Bells sounding, lights flashing—we have a winner! Unfortunately, that's not a good thing. Instead of attracting guys, you are most likely scaring them off with your aggressive behavior. Don't be so desperate for guys to notice and like you. Funnel all that energy into getting to know the only one who can fill your heart—Jesus!

MOSTLY AS: MEDIUM—There are no bells sounding yet, but if you're not careful, there could be soon. You're on the verge of becoming a full-time player in the flirting game. View this as a wake-up call, put that hammer down (or turn off the charm), and find another game. I personally recommend the one where you get to throw darts at the balloons.

MOSTLY CS: LOW—OK, so you're a wimp on the Flirt-O-Meter, but trust me, that's a good thing. You're confident in who you are and don't need a guy to make you feel better about yourself. You don't play games, and character is more important in your book. Keep right on trusting God for your future, and he will take care of all the details!

what will a guy do... for a girl?

by *Susie Davis*

My friend Lisa knew that a guy named Will was interested in dating me. She knew because on a youth group ski trip this guy named Will stood and waited for a chance to sit down next to me. I don't mean he stood waiting for a few minutes. He stood waiting for five hours. That's longer than most guys would wait for a girl so I have to tell you it captured my attention and, eventually, he captured my heart.

Lisa and I had decided that we would sit next to each other on the long, all-day bus trip to our snow-ski destination. It was about fifteen hours from Austin, Texas to Breckenridge, Colorado. We had our pillows, plenty of junky snacks, and an ample amount of energy to sustain us as we found our seats on the chartered bus. I picked the window seat, and Lisa took the aisle seat.

We were wildly excited and happy to be stuffed in the bus with some forty other high school kids from our church youth group. The clear goal Lisa and I had for the next week was to have fun and lots of it.

Our determination to have fun was only matched by Will's determination to have the seat Lisa was sitting in so that he could talk with me. About an hour after the bus departed, Will came and stood next to Lisa. He stood in the aisle and talked and talked and talked. Standing and standing and standing. Waiting and waiting and waiting. Until finally the break he was looking for appeared. Lisa excused herself to go the bathroom, and when she did, Will snapped up the opportunity and sat down next to me.

Now, I don't have to tell you I was absolutely thrilled to have Will sit down next to me. He was tall, dark, and handsome; and to top it off, he was a standout Christian guy. Two years older than me, he was a leader in the youth group. He played football at a local high school. He water-skied competitively. He was well liked by others—and by me.

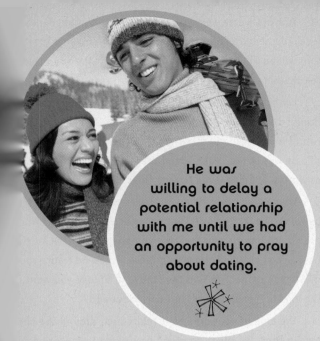

> He was willing to delay a potential relationship with me until we had an opportunity to pray about dating.

own while a selfish person is always thinking of ways to satisfy their own needs. Will was willing to suffer on my behalf and make sure my reputation was protected. He was willing to delay a potential relationship with me until we had an opportunity to pray about dating. Quite simply, he was willing to wait.

How many times can you think of a situation when a high school guy deferred going out with you to make sure it was God's will? Conversely, think for a minute about the times you have heard a guy say to you or one of your friends, "If you *really loved me,* you would _____ with me." Oh really? You know what? That's not how God defines love. It is certainly not the way Paul has described love in the Bible. Deep in your gut, you know that guys who pressure

By the time Lisa returned to her seat, Will and I were deep in conversation so (with a discreet smile my direction) she wandered down the aisle to find another seat. Meanwhile, Will and I talked for hours. We talked about school stuff. We talked about the ski trip. And we talked about God. The trip turned out to be great for both of us. That said, you can probably do the math and figure out that by the time the trip was over, Will and I were an item. But not in the way you are probably thinking. As much as we wanted to be together and as much as we would have liked to think of ourselves as a couple, Will insisted that we wait to get back to Austin and pray about dating. He didn't want people to think that it was just a fling, and he was concerned about that. So the entire trip had this theme around waiting. Will waited to talk to me on the bus. We both decided on waiting to begin the dating process and define the relationship. I have to tell you that the waiting was not much fun. There was some suffering going on. Long-suffering—which is another word for *patience.*

In 1 Corinthians 13, the apostle Paul defines what love looks like, and he starts by stating that love is patient. And honestly, patience is a really good test to determine whether or not a guy loves you because patience in action is selflessness. A selfless person puts others' needs before his

and push are not really valuing you. Rather, they are putting themselves first. When a guy comes up with a line like that, a really great response might be, "If you really loved *me* you would wait. And wait and wait. Because love is *patient*."

Now while that type of response is likely to illicit a snide remark from most high school guys, I do want you to take away some truth from this whole concept.

The truth is this:

> Love is patient; love is kind. Love does not envy;
> is not boastful; is not conceited;
> does not act improperly; is not selfish;
> is not provoked; does not keep a record of wrongs;
> finds no joy in unrighteousness, but rejoices in the truth;
> bears all things, believes all things,
> hopes all things, endures all things.
> Love never ends. (1 Corinthians 13:4–8a)

You are worth someone loving you with that kind love. You need to know that God has a man in mind for y that will be willing to love you in his way. Please don't sett for anything other than God's very best for your life.

I taught a Bible study for high school girls, and the o thing I continually urged them to do was to pray for the future husbands, whether they thought they already kne who he was or not. I also urged them to think of themselve as worthy of being loved beyond their wildest imagination

What will a boy do for a girl? Better yet, what will a bo be willing to do for you? What are your expectations? Who are you willing to wait for? Are you going to settle for th first guy who comes along regardless of how he treats you Or will you agree with God that the kind of love you want i the kind of love described in 1 Corinthians 13?

The man of your dreams is really right around the cor ner. In fact, he might be standing around just waiting fo the chance to talk to you. Because you know what? The tall dark, handsome guy I got to know on that youth group sk trip, the one exhibiting patience on my behalf, is the mar I am married to today. ✶

Can You Relate?

1. If you are dating a guy right now, would he be willing to exhibit some "long-suffering" on your behalf?

2. What are your highest expectations for the "man of your dreams"?

3. List some of the attributes you expect from a guy you would like to date.

4. List some of the attributes you think God expects from a guy he would like you to date.

5. How do the lists from questions 3 and 4 compare?

6. Begin a prayer list for your future husband. Keep it in a journal and look over it occasionally to make sure you are looking for God's best for your life.

We Asked...You TOLD:
your comments about...
GUYS

survey question: **What confuses you about guys?**

The type of girls they like. —Brooke, 13

When they ignore you when they truly like you. —Deborah, 14

The way they think. Why can't they just try to understand our emotions instead of question them? —Lauren, 16

Sometimes they think it's cool to get in trouble or get a bad grade on a test or something. When I get bad grades, it's punishment for me! —Grace, 12

Why some want to date trashy girls. —Emily, 14

I get confused when guys give mixed signals. Everything seems to be going well, and you always think they like you. But then they'll make some comment to someone else, like that you're immature or annoying. You never know what is really running through their heads. —Sarah, 14

Why they can't just tell you how they feel instead of having to be "Mister Macho"? I guess it's a guy thing. —Stephanie, 17

Guys! Oh wow, they are the most confusing thing ever (besides math). Sometimes they can be nice and sweet and funny, and other times they are a pain in the neck! —Linley, 13

I don't understand why guys act like something doesn't bother them when it really does! —Jana, 15

How they think we're more confusing than they are! —Suzanne, 17

They are always trying to stand out and be weird by making faces in class. —Perry, 12

I don't get how some are attracted to mean girls. —Lacie, 17

One day a guy may talk and have fun with you, then the next day it's like he goes out of his way to ignore you! What's up with that!? —April, 12

It's like torturing them if you ask what they think or how they feel. —Lauren, 15

Some don't think they need to comb their hair. —Rebecca, 15

Why there can't be more godly ones? —Brittany, 16

Why they won't think about the way they feel. —Elisabeth, 17

How sometimes they're different around their guy friends than when they are around you. —Jaime, 14

They're so simple and yet so complex at the same time. —Hannah, 14

It's rare to find a mature, Christian boy nowadays. It wouldn't kill them to get off their electronics every once in awhile! —Paige, 15

Why don't they just tell a girl when they like her instead of waiting for her to tell them? —Alyssa, 14

I go to a small private school, and I just don't understand why a lot of the guys at our school have "favorites." There are about five girls that they ALWAYS do stuff with, and it's not like the rest of us girls are shy or rude or anything. Why can't we all just be friends? —Taylor, 15

How they seem to like you, but then all of a sudden, they totally ignore you, and you're wondering, what was THAT all about? —Brittany, 15

Why do guys pierce their ears, wear baggy clothes, or make loud body noises? Do they think this *attracts* girls!? —Kendra, 16 ✱

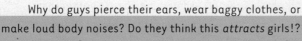

Hold out or Make out

by Vicki Courtney

On a recent afternoon while driving my youngest son Hayden (sixth grade), home from school, he caught me off guard with this question, "Mom, how old were you when you had your first kiss?" I hesitated to tell him, given the fact it was at his same age.

His question brought the memory back in an instant. I was with a group of friends at the movies and sitting next to Bobby Mallow, sixth-grade popular boy, and rumor had it, a kissing bandit. He had recently asked me to "go steady," which is the same thing as "going out" today. I was busy chatting with my friend on the other side of me when the lights in the theater dimmed. I was focused on the previews when all of a sudden, Bobby reached over and grabbed my hand. As the movie wore on, I noticed Bobby beginning to lean into me more and more, finally to where the sides of our heads were almost touching. Just as I was beginning to wonder what his motives were in leaning in so close, he let go of my hand and quickly put his arm around me. That was a new feeling. Before I had time to analyze this move, he turned toward me and with his other hand reached over and gently touched the back of my head, making it nearly impossible to escape the kiss that followed. As if I wanted to, anyway. What happened next was a tingle down-to-your-toes, can't-catch-your-breath, movie-star kiss. Fortunately, we both thought movie stars kissed with their mouths closed so it stayed rather innocent.

marriage is outlawed in all fifty states. If you get caught, y[ou] could do serious jail time." Not buying it, he replied, "[...] Mom. I just wanted to know how old you were—that's a[ll.]"

Then it occurred to me what a blessing it was th[at] he would even consider discussing the topic of a fir[st] kiss with me. And at that point I decided to take [the] risk, and I told him the truth.

"Hayden, do you really want to know how old I w[as] when I had my first kiss?" He nodded his head and I pro-ceeded to tell him. I told him how it made me feel, an[d] I confessed that my heart would still race days and eve[n] weeks later at the mere thought of that kiss.

> I stored that kiss in the back of my mind and would replay it from time to time. It has been thirty years since that kiss and I can still remember it in detail as if it were yesterday.

When it was over, I was certain that my heart was beating loud enough for everyone in that theater to hear. I felt as if I was floating on air in some sort of half-awake, half-asleep state of mind. We broke up before a next kiss, and some time passed before I kissed another boy. In the meantime, I stored that kiss in the back of my mind and would replay it from time to time. It has been thirty years since that kiss, and I can still remember it in detail as if it were yesterday.

As I was reflecting back on my first kiss, I heard Hayden calling me back to reality. "Mom, Mom, did you hear me? When was your first kiss?" I snapped out of my trance-like journey to the past and replied to Hayden, "Why are you asking? You are far too young to worry about such silly things!" Wow, that should sway him from taking my same path, huh?

I happened to know that he liked a girl who, rumor had it, liked him in return. I also happened to know that they were both invited to a bonfire party that weekend. And with that thought, my mind raced back to a few bon-fires I had attended . . . and hayrides . . . and school dances. Yikes. I had no choice but to head this off at the pass.

"Hayden, I know you probably don't know this, but kissing before

As much as I didn't want to tell him, I leveled with him and told him it was perfectly normal for a kid his age to be curious about kissing and maybe even want to kiss. I also

told him that I was far too young for that kiss and the emotions that followed. I told him that the earlier you kiss, the more you dwell on the next kiss, and the next, and the next. After awhile, kissing becomes less and less special, and eventually you look for other ways to get that same thrill—things that should be saved for marriage. He seemed to be listening, and hopefully he will learn from his mother's mistake.

A kiss is special, and chances are, you will never forget your first kiss. If you haven't had your first kiss and feel like you are the only one left among your friends, keep in mind that only a little over half of thirteen to sixteen year olds have kissed someone romantically. That means that almost half have not, so you are not alone.[1] Whether you have kissed or not, it's important to remember that a kiss is not something to be given away casually. Girls who are willing to make out just for the sake of making out are often branded as "easy." Do you want to be thought of that way? Kisses should be guarded, treasured, and shared sparingly. They are too precious to be shared in the backseat of a car, in a dark theater, or at the spin of a bottle.

Years from now, when you meet your future husband, do you really want to tell him that you lost count on how many guys you kissed over the years? Ick. Believe it or not, I actually know of a few couples that saved their first kiss for their wedding day. While it is rare to make it that long, the longer you can wait to kiss and the fewer kisses you give out over time, chances are, the more special it will be when you kiss your future husband. Remember in *Princess Diaries* when Mia imagined that her first kiss would make her foot pop? When the boy she liked kissed her, it wasn't at all what she had hoped for. She discovered that there is much more to a sincere kiss than two people being "in like." By the end of the movie, she finally got her wish of a foot-popping kiss, and it was with someone she had gotten to know first as a friend. Now stop and ask yourself this question: Do you think we would have liked her character as much had she been the type to give kisses out like candy to any guy that looks her way? No way! What made her character endearing was her obvious innocence and self-respect.

A kiss is intimate and personal. Kissing is not a spo[rt?] While other girls are making out with countless guys, choo[se] to hold out for that special foot-popping kiss. Your futu[re] husband will be glad you did. The fewer guys he has [to] measure himself against, the better. Guard your kisses, a[nd] above all, guard your heart (Proverbs 4:23). ✳

—————————————————

1. NBC News and

Can You Relate?

1. What do you think about **making ou[t] just for the sake of making out?**

2. Every girl should go before God an[d] come up with a plan about **how far is too far in a relationship.** Do you have such a plan?

3. Why do you think it's hard for couples to **draw a line at kissing and not go any further?**

4. What advice would you give Christian girls who are in serious dating relationships and discover that they are **not able to stop at kissing?** Would you advise them to stop? Would you be able to if you were in their shoes?

your ❀ relationship with... Friends

With FRIENDS like that

by Whitney Prosperi

Do you remember a time when you realized that a "friend" wasn't quite a real friend? I do. It's a long, crazy story, and trust me, if you could see a videotape of the small catastrophe, you would laugh your head off. Unfortunately, I didn't have a video camera, but if I had, you can bet I would be a millionaire right now.

To make a long (and humiliating) story short, when Tammy got some speed going, she jumped up on the metal rail under the cart and started to coast. You probably did this when you were a kid. So did I. Well, here's a health tip for free: when you're in college, you are no longer light enough for the cart to hold your weight. The end of the cart tipped

Real friends are sometimes hard to find, but when you discover one, you have received one of God's best gifts.

One afternoon when I was in college, my friend Tammy and I went to the grocery store to stock up on snacks and necessities. Before we even began our shopping trip, we started goofing around. She is one of those friends that brings out the fun in everyone, and before long we were speeding the length of the store with our shopping cart. Let me state right now that I am not suggesting that we used sane judgment or that anyone should ever try this on a similar shopping excursion.

up, and she fell headfirst into the basket. Next, the shopping cart (with her inside) turned upside down. It was now completely flipped over and careening toward the deli meat counter, which was behind a glass case. No kidding!

As you can imagine, most people in the store turned their heads to see a redhead flying by the checkout lines in the basket of an upside-down grocery cart. Honestly, it was one of the funniest things I have ever seen. And also the scariest. In case you're wondering about the glass case and my friend's overall health, she and the deli meat made it just

e. Her hands, which were drug under the weight of the basket (with her in it), were cut and bruised. And of course she was obably more embarrassed than she had ever been before.

If you can believe it, now comes the most disturbing part of the story. After Tammy and her racing cart came to a halt nd while I was helping her climb out and stand up, we noticed one of our other friends a few aisles away staring at us. We new she had noticed us because, at this point, everyone in the store had, so we waved at her. And guess what? She literally ted like she didn't see us and walked the other way. She was ashamed to admit she knew us.

Ever had a similar experience? I'm not talking about the shopping cart ride or almost crashing into a glass meat coun- r. I'm wondering if you have ever thought someone was your friend, but when you did something that embarrassed her, she umped you and turned the other way. We've all been there. It's painful, and I'm talking about more than bruised hands and stiff back.

Real friends are sometimes hard to find, but when you discover one, you have received one of God's best gifts. How do u know if you've got an authentic, stick-with-you-through-it-all kind of friend? See if she matches up to God's definition f an authentic friend found in his Word.

1 Stands with you through good and bad times.

Everyone wants to be your friend when you make the cheerleading squad or score a date with Mr. Wonderful. But what about if you get dumped or you trip in the lunchroom? How about when you stand up for the right thing even though it's the unpopular deci- sion? Will your friend support you, or will she laugh and go the way of the crowd? A true friend sticks with you even though it may not be a convenient or popular choice.

"A friend loves at all times."
(Proverbs 17:17)

2 Respects you enough to protect what you tell her.

Ever had a friend who can't keep her mouth shut? About an hour after you tell her something, she has broadcast it to about twenty other people. Then before you know it, everyone in your school district knows your private busi- ness. Trust is a vital trait found in authentic friends. Ask God to bring you a friend who will keep the big and small.

"Whoever conceals an offense promotes love, but whoever gossips about it separates friends." (Proverbs 17:9)

3 Makes choices based on the wisdom of God.

A true friend won't ask you to compromise what you believe. She will encourage you to make the right choice rather than tempt you to make the wrong one. She will choose based on what's wise rather than on what's popular. This kind of friend is crucial because, as the Bible says, you become like the people you spend time with.

> **"The one who walks with the wise will become wise, but a companion of fools will suffer harm."**
> **(Proverbs 13:20)**

4 Encourages you in your spiritual walk.

A real friend challenges you to follow Christ. She knows that you'll be happiest and most fulfilled when your purpose is to pursue God. She prays for you, shares what she's learning from God's Word, and encourages you to put him first. This kind of friend will help you stay on track and spur you on in your own walk with Christ.

> **"Iron sharpens iron, and one man sharpens another."**
> **(Proverbs 27:17)**

Now take a few minutes to think about the kind of friend you are. Are you the type who stands with your friends, even when it's not easy to do? Do you encourage them to follow the narrow road that Jesus calls us to? Are you trustworthy? Take a few minutes to pray that you will be a genuine friend. Remember what your mother always told you: you have to be a friend to have a friend. Focus on becoming the kind of friend you would like to have. That's a good place to start.

Can you Relate?

1. Have you ever felt the sting of rejection from someone you thought was your friend? If so, how did it make you feel?

2. Has a friend ever supported you when you stood up for what was right? Tell what happened.

3. When looking for a friend, how important is the quality of trustworthiness? Explain your answer.

4. Think of your closest friends. Do they encourage you to walk with God or tempt you to go your own way?

5. What changes will you make in your own life that would make you a better friend?

8 FRIENDSHIP FIXERS

by Susie Davis

Your friends are some of the important people in your life. You spend endless hours a week with them. You laugh with them, you share secrets with them, and you cry with them. As a result, it is important to take care of those relationships. And as in every relationship in life, things come up that cause problems. Below you will find eight things you can do to improve your friendships right now. And even if your friendships don't need fixing, you might want to read on and make sure that you have the necessary information to be the best friend ever. Think of this as a guide to keeping your friends "good friends."

it's much easier to think about yourself. But **PHILIPPIAN[S] 2:4 SAYS, "EVERYONE SHOULD LOOK OUT NOT ONLY FOR H[IS] OWN INTERESTS, BUT ALSO FOR THE INTERESTS OF OTHERS[.]"** One of my good friends gave me an idea on how she man[ages] to fight selfishness. It's called the "second cookie["]concept, and it goes something like this: Let's say th[at] you and your friend are at your house and your mom ha[s] just made her famous and delicious homemade cookie[s]. Your mom hands you the plate. What do you do? Well, [if] you want to be selfless, you let your friend pick first, and yo[u] take the "second cookie." But let's say that your friend ask[s] you to take one first, then what? If that is the case, ho[w] about choosing the smallest cookie? Or the "second" choic[e] cookie. That is how you put others' interest first; you g[o] second. And that translates into other areas besides jus[t] cookies. What about choosing to let your friend pick a res-taurant or movie instead of you? Or maybe let your frien[d] borrow those extra-cute earrings you were saving for your-self? Maybe you could even give them to her, just because. Whatever comes up with your friend, think of how you can honor her by taking second and going second.

Be Selfless...

OK, let's be honest. Most people think of themselves first. It's natural, and it comes easy. Whether you are at school or competing in your favorite sport,

Be a Secret Keeper...

This should be a no-brainer, especially for girls; but for [so]me reason it is especially hard just to keep our mouths [shu]t when it comes to keeping secrets. **PROVERBS 11:13** [ST]ATES, **"A GOSSIP GOES AROUND REVEALING A SECRET, [BU]T THE TRUSTWORTHY KEEPS A CONFIDENCE."** This doesn't [re]quire much explanation. Just a question: Are you trust[wo]rthy? If you want good friends, you must be a good friend [an]d that means you need to be trustworthy. Don't give away [se]crets that are not yours to give. When a person shares [a]secret, she trusts you with a little piece of her heart. If [yo]u are revealing secrets, you're a gossip and "a gossip [se]parates friends" (Proverbs 16:28). Do you want to fix [yo]ur friendship? Determine now to keep your mouth sealed [wh]en your friend's heart is revealed. (If your friend shares [a]secret that she is engaging in behaviors that are harm[fu]l to her, take a look at the article, "SOS! My Friend Needs [H]elp!")

Be an Encourager...

There are lots of ways to be an encourager in your friend's life. One is to tell your friend when she is good at something. Or comment on how great she looks in a new outfit. Another way to encourage is to do things for her that you know she would like or buy her a small gift or help her with homework or even her chores at home. Be creative in inspiring your friend. Think of ways to spur her on to do the things she has to do and wants to do. These are all practical ways to boost a friend's spirit and encourage them. But another (and this one can be hard, especially with your best friend) is to give your friend the freedom to enjoy other people. Don't be possessive. If she is invited to go to the mall with another person, don't make her feel bad about it. Instead, tell her to have a good time. (You can take the opportunity

to make plans by calling another friend to do something else.) But remember to let her have space to be with other people. Nothing will kill a friendship like possessiveness. Don't smother your best friend. Think of your friend as a gift from God—don't crush the gift.

Be Open to Truth from Your Friend...

"THE WOUNDS OF A FRIEND ARE TRUSTWORTHY" (PROVERBS 27:6). While the wounds of an enemy are meant to harm, wounds from a friend are often needed for our well-being. I will never forget what happened to me when my best friend wounded me.

During my freshman year in high school, I had gotten into a bad habit of using God's name in vain. Instead of saying, "Oh my gosh," I would say, "Oh my God." I obviously

> Nothing will kill a friendship like possessiveness. Don't smother your best friend. Think of your friend as a gift from God—don't crush the gift.

didn't think it was too big a deal, but fortunately for me, my friend Stacy did. We were together at a football game, and we had decided to go to the concession stand and get a drink. While we were waiting in line, she looked at me and said, "Susie, why do you use God's name in vain all the time?" She startled me with the question, but the way she asked the question was not accusatory; it was honest. And so I responded with, "I don't know why I am doing that, but I know I shouldn't." It wasn't fun for me to have to answer Stacy's question, and I'm sure it wasn't fun for her to have to ask it, but that wound helped me to break an unhealthy habit that was breaking one of God's commands. And I am so grateful she was willing to ask the hard question and wound my heart to help me readjust my thinking back to honoring God with my words. (CHECK OUT DEUTERONOMY 5:11 FOR MORE ON MISUSING THE NAME OF GOD.)

Be Supportive...

Did you know that even Jesus needed supportive friends? When Jesus was grappling with the fact that he was going to die, he called out a few of his best friends to help him out. MARK 14:33–34 RECORDS: "HE TOOK PETER, JAMES, AND JOHN WITH HIM, AND HE BEGAN TO BE DEEPLY DISTRESSED AND HORRIFIED. THEN HE SAID TO THEM, 'MY SOUL IS SWALLOWED UP IN SORROW—TO THE POINT OF DEATH. REMAIN HERE AND STAY AWAKE.'" Jesus called out the best. I call them his "garden friends" because he took them to the Garden of Gethsemane where he asked them to remain with him and stay awake. We all need "garden friends." They are the people in your life that help you through your darkest hour. And as much as we need "garden friends" we

should seek to be "garden friends." If your best friend going through an especially rough time, you might be call upon to be that kind of friend. It is not always easy, a it might not be especially fun, but to be able to suppor friend in a hard situation is to be like Jesus.

Be Willing to Forgive..

You know the really crazy thing about friends and eve "garden friends"? They can let you down. Jesus' "garde friends" let him down by falling asleep in his greatest hou of need. So it is wise to keep in mind that your friend will hurt your feelings sometimes. And since it is going to

> It is not always easy and it might not be especially fun, but to be able to support a friend in a hard situation is to be like Jesus.

happen, you need a way to fix the problem. God designed a way to handle the inevitable wrecked relationship, and it's called forgiveness. "JUST AS THE LORD HAS FORGIVEN YOU, SO ALSO YOU MUST FORGIVE" (COLOSSIANS 3:13). Not fun but necessary. Forgiveness is a healthy part of every relationship, friendship included. If you are unable to get over the fact that someone has hurt you or let

...down, the Bible gives a clear indication of what's ...ead. **PROVERBS 17:9 PROMISES, "OVERLOOK AN OFFENSE ...D BOND A FRIENDSHIP; FASTEN ON TO A SLIGHT AND— ...OD-BYE, FRIEND"** *(THE MESSAGE)*. The important part of ...endship is the ability to love, and love releases offense. ...e kind of love God talks about is love without condition. ... to fix a friendship, you must learn to love when you are ...rt and to love when you are happy. It's easy to love your ...ends when you are enjoying them. It's easy to be nice to ...em when you are having fun with them. But what about the ...mes when they hurt your feelings? Or what about the times ...en they cancel plans and leave you out? What about the ...mes when your friends talk about you behind your back? It ...ppens. Those are the times that it is really hard, and you ...ight be tempted to hang on to an offense. But just as God ...as forgiven us, we must be willing to forgive others. He can ...ve you what you need to keep being a good friend even ... your friend is mistreating you. During those times your ...iends are absolutely driving you crazy, consider praying ...nd asking God to give you wisdom about how to handle the ...tuation.

To have healthy relationships we need to strive toward the guidelines God gives.

end up feeling drained and overwhelmed if your friendship is unbalanced. The key to balance in all relationships is making Christ the center. Lean on God and let him meet your deepest needs; after that you will be in a place to have healthy relationships with your friends.

Be Well-Balanced...

Your friends cannot and should not meet all of your needs. While we all need the support of our friends, don't expect your friends to fix all of your problems. There is only so much one person can do, and if you lean into your friends for everything, chances are you are going to end up disappointed and frustrated. It's likely that your friends will

Be a "Jesus" Friend...

The foundation for any great friendship is the ability to give the kind of love Jesus demonstrates toward you. **IN JOHN 15:12 JESUS SAID, "THIS IS MY COMMAND: LOVE ONE ANOTHER AS I HAVE LOVED YOU."** Jesus has set the standard, and while we won't always react the way we should, to have healthy relationships we need to strive toward the guidelines God gives. **TAKE A LOOK AT**

1 CORINTHIANS 13:4–7 AS A CHECKLIST FOR A HOW-TO ON FRIENDSHIP: "LOVE NEVER GIVES UP. LOVE CARES MORE FOR OTHERS THAN FOR SELF. LOVE DOESN'T WANT WHAT IT DOESN'T HAVE. LOVE DOESN'T STRUT, DOESN'T HAVE A SWELLED HEAD, DOESN'T FORCE ITSELF ON OTHERS, ISN'T ALWAYS "ME FIRST," DOESN'T FLY OFF THE HANDLE, DOESN'T KEEP SCORE OF THE SINS OF OTHERS, DOESN'T REVEL WHEN OTHERS GROVEL, TAKES PLEASURE IN THE FLOWERING OF TRUTH, PUTS UP WITH ANYTHING, TRUSTS GOD ALWAYS, ALWAYS LOOKS FOR THE BEST, NEVER LOOKS BACK, BUT KEEPS GOING TO THE END" (THE MESSAGE).

Fix your friendship by acting like Jesus would have you act, and you will be a great friend. While the world may have many interesting definitions for love, Jesus topped the[m] all in a practical way. He said in John 15:13, "No one h[as] greater love than this, that someone would lay down his l[ife] for his friends." Did you know that Jesus did that just [for] you? He literally laid his life on the line for you so that y[ou] could have eternal life and a relationship with God. You w[ill] find no better friend than Jesus Christ. He will never st[op] loving you. He will never stop caring for you. He will nev[er] run out of time for you. Never. As friends in your life co[me] and go, Jesus Christ remains the same yesterday, today, a[nd] forever. And because of that promise, you can count on h[is] consistent and loving friendship throughout your life. So g[et] to know him well, and as you do, you will find he is the be[st] friend ever.✶

Can You Relate?

1. Can you think of a way to be selfless with your best friend? Make a short list of ideas that put your friend first and you second.

2. Can you identify a time when gossip separated two friends? Consider memorizing Proverbs 16:28 as a way to help you remember that sharing secrets wrecks friendships.

3. Write down some ways you can encourage one of your friends this week. Now pray for the time and energy to accomplish it.

4. Have you ever been wounded by a friend that told you the truth about a situation in your life? How did it positively impact your life? If you have never thanked her for that, consider giving her a call or writing her a note and thanking her.

5. Do you have any "garden friends"? How have they gotten you through any hard times? If you don't have people in your life that you would consider "garden friends," pray that God will show you some; and when he does, don't forget to thank him!

6. Do you need to forgive one of your friends for hurting you? Pray that God would help you not to hold on to an offense. If you are able, call your friend and tell her that the past is the past and you are no longer holding anything against her. It will heal your friendship.

7. Do you have a tendency to expect too much from your friends? How can you lighten up and lean into God instead?

8. Write down 1 Corinthians 13:4–7 on a note card and carry it with you for several weeks. Read it several times every day. By the end of that time, you will be well on your way to remembering God's kind of love in the important relationships in your life.

by Whitney Prosperi

off the deep end

Do you remember when you were younger, and *wild* meant watching a bad TV show now and then? Maybe the "bad crowd" said curse words or talked back to teachers. But now that you're older, *bad* can be really bad. Some of the friends you have known most of your life may choose to walk completely away from the way they were raised and the things they professed.

Chances are high that as you've read these words, someone you know has come to mind. Maybe this friend, or group of friends, used to have a different lifestyle. You might be thinking of some students in your youth group or just some friends you know at school. Whatever the case, this group has taken a different road. Maybe your friends made a commitment to save sex until marriage but then later seemed to throw that decision out the window. Or maybe you had agreed that your group wouldn't drink or try drugs, but all that has changed now. They have gone off the deep end it seems.

Do you feel that you are the only one who remembers the vows you made and the teaching you heard? Do you stand alone in a crowd that seems determined to want to fall—or rather jump headlong—into sin? If so, we'll look at some ways you can find strength to stand and even to influence a group to change.

The first thing you have to do is take
[car]e of yourself. While that may sound
[self]ish, it's true. If you've been on an
[airp]lane lately, you probably remember
[the] flight attendant showing passengers
[the] standard safety information. While
[you], like most everyone else, probably
[did]n't pay much attention, he or she
[sai]d something absolutely crucial.
[(Li]sten up! This may save your life some-
[da]y.) "If the cabin pressure changes,
[oxy]gen masks will drop down. If you
[are] sitting next to someone who needs
[as]sistance, place the mask over your
[ow]n head first, then help the one who
[ne]eds aid." It's such great advice for
[lif]e. How in the world can you help some-
[on]e else if you aren't getting the oxygen
[yo]u need? You can't. And you can't help
[a] friend who is wandering into a maze
[of] sin unless you are securely con-
[n]ected to the life-giving presence of
[Je]sus.

So make sure that even though
[th]e pull of the crowd is to forsake
[Ch]rist, you stay in the Word and pray.
[R]emember that you also are susceptible
[t]o the lure of sin. First
[C]orinthians 10:12–13
[s]ays, "Therefore, who-
[e]ver thinks he stands
[m]ust be careful not to
[f]all! No temptation has
[o]vertaken you except
[w]hat is common to
[h]umanity. God is faithful
[a]nd He will not allow you
[t]o be tempted beyond
[w]hat you are able, but
[w]ith the temptation He
[w]ill also provide a way of
[e]scape, so that you are able to bear it." Watch out for pride.
[I]t can rear its ugly head and convince you that you would
[n]ever get caught in the snares of sin. But as soon as you
[b]ecome casual in the fight to live a pure life, you are fair
[g]ame. That's when you will find yourself walking down some
[o]f those same roads of destruction.

> Make sure that even
> though the pull of the
> crowd is to forsake
> Christ, you stay in the
> Word and pray.

Next you want to make sure you have a support system.
Find a friend who shares your desire to make godly
choices. You may even join together once a
week to pray and encourage each other.
Ask your youth minister or a leader to
hold you accountable in the decisions

Find a friend who shares your desire to make godly choices, and join together once a week to pray and encourage each other.

you make. Make sure you surround yourself with friends who desire to walk with Christ. If you don't have many, pray that God would bring you some and then watch for him to do it. They may not be whom you would have expected, but they will help you find the support you need to stay strong.

Finally, don't write off your friends who are making sinful choices. While you will need to put some distance between you and them, make sure they know you still care about them. Let them know that you pray for them and are always willing to help or listen if they need anything. You'll also want to express your concern over the choices they've made. Pray about this conversation and then tell them how you are concerned for the consequences they may have to bear. Remind them that God is always ready to forgive and change a repentant heart.

There is a fine line between reaching out to a friend who has chosen a sinful path and being tempted by them to take that route too. Make sure that you are the one influencing them and not the other way around. Galatians 6:1 says, "Brothers, if someone is caught in any wrongdoing, you who are spiritual should restore such a person with a gentle spirit, watching out for yourselves so you won't be tempted also." Be careful to offer support to your friend without putting yourself in situations where you will be tempted to compromise. The fact that you have taken a stand for what is right may just help your friend, or someone in a group gone bad, have the courage to come back to God.*

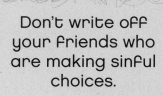

Don't write off your friends who are making sinful choices.

1. Have you ever had a friend or group of friends head down a wild path? If so, how did that make you feel?

2. What are some practical things you can do to make sure you stay connected to Jesus when you're trying to help a friend who has made bad choices?

3. List some people that can serve as a support system to you so you don't get lured into sinful behaviors. What can they do to help you keep the commitments you've made to Christ?

4. Is there someone you need to confront about sinful choices she has been making? If so, when will you have this conversation with her, and what will you say?

5. Is it time for you to put some distance between you and a friend? If so, pray about how you will do this by honoring truth while also acting in love.

10 Never Ever Evers

❶ **Never ever** gossip about your friends.

❷ **Never ever** turn your back on a good friend just to be popular.

❸ **Never ever** expect that your friend, even your closest friend, will never hurt your feelings.

❹ **Never ever** fail to forgive a friend.

❺ **Never ever** expect one friend to meet all your needs.

❻ **Never ever** ignore a friend intentionally.

❼ **Never ever** laugh at your friend.

❽ **Never ever** forget to celebrate with your friends.

❾ **Never ever** neglect to spend time with your friends.

❿ **Never ever** belittle a friend's feelings.

ONLINE DIARIES:
ARE YOU SHARING TMI?

by Vicki Courtney

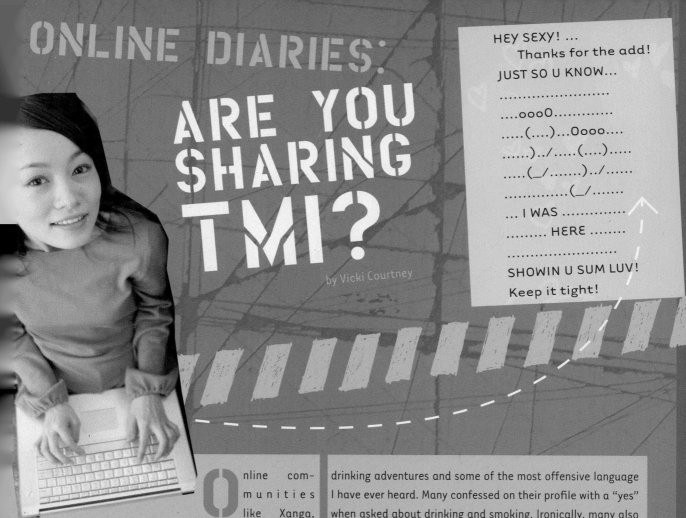

HEY SEXY! ...
    Thanks for the add!
JUST SO U KNOW...
....
....oooO.............
.....(....)...Oooo....
......)../.....(....).....
.....(_/.......)../......
..............(_/.......
... I WAS ....
.... HERE ....
....
SHOWIN U SUM LUV!
Keep it tight!

O nline communities like Xanga, LiveJournal, and MySpace are all the rage. As you probably know already, the sites allow you to create your own communities where you can share photos, journals, and interests with a network of friends . . . and strangers. While the sites caution against uploading inappropriate comments and images, one glance at the sites indicates that few rules are being enforced. I was tipped off to MySpace by a concerned mother who shared a heartbreaking story about a "good girl" in their youth group who had uploaded inappropriate pictures of herself on the site. She informed me that it was the new rage among the teens in her area to create online profiles with a photo album and journal. When the word spread about the girl in the youth group, most parents had absolutely no idea that such a forum existed. Many were further shocked to discover their own kids on the site.

Out of curiosity, I logged onto the site, created an identity, and ran a group search by plugging in the name of the high school where my own kids attend. I was stunned to find pictures of students downing vodka straight from the bottle, a popular girl posing in her black lace bra and panties, sexually crude remarks and comments posted that detailed weekend drinking adventures and some of the most offensive language I have ever heard. Many confessed on their profile with a "yes" when asked about drinking and smoking. Ironically, many also filled in "Christian" on the profile when asked about religion.

Some kids had more than five hundred friends with their respective thumbnail pictures that they had added to their home page. Some of the pictures were of girls baring cleavage or posing in thong underwear. I was struck by the cavalier and carefree attitudes that many of the students displayed on the site. It was as if they imagined that parents were somehow blocked from accessing the site.

Recent news accounts have reported that parents are not the only ones who are accessing the sites for more information about their teens. I recently read an account of a teacher at a private middle school in San Francisco who discovered that many of the middle school students were going onto the MySpace.com site and others like it during school hours and updating their profiles and blogs. She stated, "These sites are like a candy store for predators. Especially since the kids actually, truly believe that their journals are 'private.' They struggle with the concept that NOTHING is private about posting to the Web."[1]

The school ultimately printed out a hard copy of the profiles of each and every student who had used the site during school hours and attached a disciplinary notice to it and handed it over to students and their parents. When confronted with a hard copy of their profiles, many of the students were shocked and angry that school officials had viewed their pages on the site. One student even accused the teacher of invading her privacy! The students actually assumed that it was impossible for adults to penetrate their perceived private online world! *Perceived* is the key word here. Nothing is private on the World Wide Web!

> "These blog sites are like a candy store for predators. Especially since the kids actually, truly believe that their journals are private."

Another news account noted that these types of sites are the new hangouts for predators. A detective in Plano, Texas, said that in five minutes of searching Xanga, he found personal information about Plano children that a predator could use to get close to them. He said blogs quickly give predators information that would take weeks or months to gather from talking to kids in a chatroom.[2] It wouldn't be hard for a predator or stalker to put two and two together from the journal entries and pictures and track down victims. Think it can't happen to you? Think again. Consider the following real-life account from a mother:

"I found a message in my [16-year-old] daughter's MySpace.com mailbox from someone saying, 'You are a doll. We should get together.' I googled the e-mail address he left, and it turned out to be a guy who produces pornography, specializing in teenage girls. He purposely left the message in the MySpace mailbox (password-protected), rather than leaving it as a comment [or post in her blog], where anyone could see it."

The mother reported what she found to the local police department and to CyberTipline.com. "In less than a week, I received an email from the police detective saying he had spoken with a special agent from the FBI, and they wanted to look into this immediately." Their research turned up an east coast news story about a girl being killed during a photo shoot set up by the porn producer in 2004. The person who had contacted her daughter through MySpace had just been found guilty of killing that girl.[3] Had he not been locked up, who knows how many other gullible girls in the MySpace community might have become victims.

John Shehan of the National Center for Missing & Exploited Children said, "If teens are there, predators are there too." The problem is, you can't always tell who the predators are. They know teen lingo and how ultimately to win their trust. They are masters at the game. Many times they pretend to be close to the teen's age when, in actuality, they are perverted, dirty old men.

Let me note that I did find some wholesome profiles in my blogging research. I found teens whose blogs attested

to God's greatness, highlighted their favorite passages of Scripture, and restricted their friend list to real friends, many of whom shared the same values and beliefs. Their sites did not have high traffic and multiple postings from strangers because their goal was not to build a friend base of hundreds of online friends. Blogging in and of itself is not evil, but unfortunately there will always be those who choose to use it for evil purposes.

When it comes to the community blogging sites, perhaps it would be wise to remember that there is no "my space" or "your space" because all space is his space (say that one five times really fast). First Chronicles 29:11 helps put it into perspective: "Yours, LORD, is the greatness and the power and the glory and the splendor and the majesty, for everything in the heavens and on earth belongs to You. Yours, LORD, is the kingdom, and You are exalted as head over all."

If you decide to participate in an online community, keep the following tips in mind:

Make sure you have your parents' blessing. If they give you a green light, give them a link to your site. For safety reasons alone, you shouldn't be typing any thing on your blog that you wouldn't want your parents to know.

Utilize the privacy controls and set your page to private. Your friends will still be able to locate you and send a request to be added to your friend list. Setting your page to private adds an extra level of protection. It sends a clear message to predators that you do not wish to be contacted by online strangers and that your purpose is to use the site as a means to communicate with your approved friends. Remember, this only adds a level of protection and is not 100 percent fool-proof. If a stalker or predator wants to get on your site bad enough, they can pose to be a friend.

Never share your last name, school name, church name, city, phone numbers, screen name, e-mail address, or other information that makes it easy for strangers to identify you or contact you by another means (like in person!).

I found teens whose blogs attested to God's greatness, highlighted their favorite passages of Scripture, and restricted their friend list to real friends, many of whom shared the same values and beliefs.

Read over your profile to see if you have disclosed information that would enable a stalker or predator to track you down. I know this sounds creepy, but try to view your blog objectively through the eyes of someone who may have malicious intent. You can never assume that only "good people" are viewing your profile.

Make sure your pictures are appropriate. Never upload pictures in swimsuits, pjs, or undergarments. Do not pose suggestively or seductively. It may seem funny to you, but those with malicious intent will misread it.

Limit your friend list to "real friends." Who needs nine zillion online strangers as friends, anyway? If you ask me, it's a cry for help, a flag to low self-esteem, and a sign that the people have way too much time on their hands—time that could be better spent with real friends in the real world doing good things.

One in five kids between the ages of ten and seventeen have been solicited for sex online.[4] If anyone ever makes you feel uncomfortable online, tell your parents! If you receive a sexual solicitation, copy and paste it in an e-mail and send it to CyberTipline.com.

Remember that information you delete never really goes away. The pages are archived and many are accessible free of charge to the public. Archive.org has a feature called "Wayback Machine" where you can enter a URL and it will list dates from the time the site was created to its current status. Clicking on a date will transport you back to what the page(s) looked like from the time the site was created. Every time you post something online, it is like leaving a trail of bread crumbs for anyone who might want to trace your journey back to its starting point—even though you are long gone! Keep in mind that many colleges, employers, and other organizations are searching MySpace for information about potential students or employees and may utilize this feature—it's cheaper than doing a background check!

If you decide to post your diary online, just remember that it becomes an open book, available to anyone in the World Wide Web network, which, the last time I checked, is a network of about 938,710,929 people.[5] If the thought of mom, dad, grandma, teachers, youth minister, boyfriend's mom, neighbors, school officials, potential employers, a slew of strangers, and countless creepy predators reading your diary makes you a little squeamish (or A LOT!), you might consider going back to the old-fashioned diary with a lock and key. *

Sources

1. SafeKids Net Family News, 3 June 2005, www.netfamilynews.org.

2. Jennifer Emily, "Predators Reading Teen Blogs, Too: Some Schools Ban Access to Web Sites," *The Dallas Morning News*, 4 May 2005, www.dallasnews.com/sharedcontent/dws/dn/latestnews/stories/050405dnccoxanga.72f2653a.html.

3. SafeKids Net Family News, 26 August 2005, www.netfamilynews.org.

4. Crimes against Children Research Center's Youth Internet Safety Survey.

5. See www.internetworldstats.com/stats.htm.

Can You Relate?

1. Do you keep your diary or journal online? If yes, do you think you have revealed too much information?

2. Do you think most teens are careful when posting information online, mindful that parents, teachers, and employers have access to the information? Do you think they realize it is highly likely that strangers and predators are viewing their profiles?

3. Have you witnessed disturbing profiles on sites like Xanga and MySpace? If yes, what might God have to say about these profiles?

4. Is it possible to participate in these sites without compromising your Christian values and beliefs?

5. What are the dangers in surfing these sites or adding complete strangers to a "friend list"?

Green with JEALOUSY?

Here's Help

by Whitney Prosperi

Have you ever wanted something so bad that you just couldn't stand it? We've all been there at one time or another. Maybe you wanted a boyfriend, acceptance into a club, a special pair of boots, or a car. You could picture yourself receiving the thing you wanted, and you just knew it would make you happy. Well, maybe you didn't get it. While you could live with that reality, the thing that made you crazy was that your friend did. Why her? And why not you?

Life can be cruel sometimes. The thing we really want may pass us by and seem to land in the lap of our friend. In times like those, we feel like the prayers we prayed were misdirected. You feel like reminding God of your address, even though you know he didn't forget it.

Jealousy, competition, and comparison all seem to be a part of growing up female. You rarely hear a guy talk about how he would kill for his friend's thighs. It's just not going to happen. But girls are another story. We constantly fight the comparison battle. If you think about it, our society feeds

As soon as you have a *jealous thought* rush through your mind, you have a choice. You can either embrace that thought, kind of like mental chewing gum, or you can reject it and replace it with the truth.

that sickness in so many ways. Picture with me a typical beauty pageant. It basically communicates that one girl is worthy, two are almost worthy, and the rest are losers. No wonder girls have a hard time accepting who they are.

What do you do when your friend gets something you want? Or when she has a prettier complexion, better hair, and more boys calling her number? You step back from the situation and ask God to give you his perspective. That's the only way to get out of the comparison game. And if you don't, it will eat you alive. Proverbs 27:4 says, "Fury is cruel, and anger is a flood, but who can withstand jealousy?"

Jealous thoughts are normal every now and then. You see someone thinner than you and secretly dislike her. Or your friend receives exactly what you've been hoping for, and you wish it hadn't happened to her. Sometimes you'll experience these feelings. This isn't the problem. What you do with them is the problem.

Here's what I mean. As soon as you have a jealous thought rush through your mind, you have a choice. You can either embrace that thought, kind of like mental chewing gum, or you can reject it and replace it with the truth.

Jealous thoughts are normal every now and then. You see someone thinner than you and secretly dislike her.

What do I do with those feelings of jealousy?

Say your friend gets voted to be mascot for your school. (This happened to me.) You both tried out, and both of you really wanted to win. You promised each other that whoever didn't get it would be happy for the other one, but when you lost, you felt jealousy creep into your heart. You secretly wished she wasn't so happy about her new success. (By the way, when you trip and fall on the big eagle feet as you're walking out in front of the student body, it doesn't boost your feeling of worth. Yes, that part of the story happened to me too.) You just feel jealous, and there's no denying it.

Here's where the choice comes in. What do you do with those feelings? Take them to God. Go straight to him and tell him exactly how you feel. He's not surprised because he already sees your heart. Ask him to help you love and support your friend. If you need to write him a letter, do that. Confess your feelings to him and ask him to help you choose to act as he would in the same situation.

Next, take some time to thank him for some blessings in your own life. You probably won't want to do it, but make yourself. How has God blessed you? What are some of the successes you have had this year? Thank him for some talents he has given you. What is your best attribute? Maybe you have a great sense of humor or have a lot of compassion for people. You may be a budding artist or a future veterinarian. Thank God for the unique way he put you together. When you see yourself as he sees you, you realize that there's a lot to be thankful for. Psalm 139:14 says, "I will praise You, because I have been remarkably and wonderfully made. Your works are wonderful, and I know this very well."

> "We must not become conceited, provoking one another, envying one another." (*Galatians 5:26*)

When you choose thankfulness, you begin to remove yourself from the comparison trap. That's not to say you won't envy a friend's wardrobe or popularity, but when those thoughts creep in, turn your focus immediately to him. Don't let them continue to grow. Just cut them off as soon as they pop into your mind.

There's always going to be someone prettier than you who has more stuff than you have. Trust me, as you grow older, your peers will still play the competition game. I'm still aware of it even as a young mom, but most times I just opt not to play. Even in Bible times women played it. It won't go away. But it's a losing game for all the players. You have the choice to remove yourself from the competition. Why not step out of it now so you don't get in the habit of playing. If this is a struggle for you, you may not beat it overnight, but the more you take those jealous thoughts to God and choose thankfulness instead, the less that nasty jealousy will rear its ugly head. ✱

1. When was the last time you felt jealous of your friend? What happened to provoke those feelings?

2. In what areas of your life are you tempted to compare yourself to others?

3. Why do you think bringing our jealous thoughts to God can help us escape the trap of comparison?

4. How does choosing thankfulness for the way God has made us remove us from the competition game?

5. What are some unique traits he has given you that you can choose to thank him for?

QUIZ

by Julie Shannan

are you the Real Deal

when it comes to being a friend?

Check the box next to the statements that describe your friend behavior.

☑ No matter what my social plans are on the weekend, I'll cancel in a heartbeat if one of my friends is having a hard time.

☐ Sometimes I don't ask my friends about their day because I don't have time to listen to the drama.

☐ If I'm talking with a cute guy after class, I'll ignore my buds so he doesn't get away.

☑ I give my friends encouraging notes and silly gifts to brighten up their week.

☐ I'm the last person my friends call if they need a favor because I'm so busy.

- I join in if someone makes fun of my friends when they aren't around.

- Even though one of my friends is kind of odd, I still sit by her during lunch.

- Occasionally I gossip about my friends over IM.

- If I'm at the mall with a cute guy friend, I sometimes act like I don't notice my girlfriends so they won't flirt with him.

- I stand up for my friends when someone makes fun of them, even if it means I might get teased.

- I always forget to return my friends' e-mails or text messages.

- I have a new best friend every few months.

MOSTLY PURPLE: ABSOLUTELY

Your friendships are extremely important to you. Whenever one of your friends is having a hard time, you're the first person they turn to for support. Your friends know that you truly care about their feelings. It doesn't matter what other people think about your friends; you love them and always find thoughtful ways to show them you care.

MOSTLY PINK: DEPENDS

Deep down you really want to be a good friend, but it's hard to find the time in your busy schedule. You sometimes get too wrapped up in your own world to notice what's going on in their world. Try setting a specific "friend time" to write sweet e-mails or text messages to them. Let them know how important they are to you and how glad you are to have them in your life.

MOSTLY BLUE: NOT SO MUCH

Popularity is more important to you than maintaining lasting friendships. The truth is that having a lot of acquaintances but few close friends can get lonely after a while. If you take time to get to know people beyond the surface, your friendships will be much more meaningful. Don't be afraid to open up and be real with your friends. You'll be glad you gave them a chance to see the real you!

"A FRIEND LOVES AT ALL TIMES."
PROVERBS 17:17a

SOS!

My Friend Needs Help

by Whitney Prosperi

Have you ever found out something about a friend that you really wished you didn't know? Maybe one night when she slept over at your house you found out that she battles an eating disorder or is addicted to drugs or alcohol. Or maybe she told you something in confidence and has made you swear to secrecy. Since the time you found out, you have been worried sick about her, and you haven't known what to do. Do you stay quiet, and by doing this risk your friend's seriously hurting herself? Or do you tell someone and risk losing her friendship forever?

This is perhaps one of the hardest situations friends can find themselves in. We're torn between feelings of helplessness, loyalty, and frustration. There are no easy answers, and it feels like every choice we make is the wrong one. We want to help, but in many ways our friend's problems are much bigger than we are. We don't really know what advice to give, and we're not sure she would listen even if we did know.

Do you have a friend who has chosen dangerous habits? Research tells us that one in every seventy high school students cut themselves to relieve stress and deal with inner turmoil. Others hurt themselves by burning or bruising parts of their bodies. Still others use drugs or alcohol to escape feelings of loneliness and pain. Some even make themselves pass out just for the feeling of a high it can bring. Dangerous behaviors like these all have one thing in common—the people trapped in their harmful cycle feel like they have to keep their behavior a secret.

That's where you, as the friend who knows the truth, come in. If your friend has confided in you about a habit she has that is potentially dangerous or life threatening, chances are that she has asked you to keep it secret. So what should you do? Just blatantly rat out your friend? Or tell a bunch of

> **Since the time** you found out, you have been worried sick about her, and you haven't known what to do. **Do you stay quiet**, and by doing this risk your friend seriously hurting herself? Or **do you tell someone** and risk losing her friendship forever?

people in hopes that someone will know what to do? No. First pray for God's wisdom and then move forward cautiously.

One of the first places to go for help is to someone old- and wiser who has dealt with these types of situations before. You may talk to your youth minister or a parent. Is there a youth volunteer or pastor you trust? If so, tell him or her your dilemma. He or she will give you advice in what the next step needs to be dealing with your friend.

Next you'll want to tell your friend that you have confided in this one person. She will most likely be mad, so prepare yourself. But after a little while, relief will probably rush over her when she realizes that she doesn't have to bear this painful secret on her own anymore. Obviously if your friend becomes so angry that she threatens suicide or any behavior that would hurt someone else, you'll need to get help immediately. While many times these threats are just that, you never know, and you can't take them lightly.

Once you tell an adult about your friend's dilemma, he or she can help her find a way out from the dangerous spiral she's in. It could be that she needs to enter a rehabilitation program or maybe just attend a support group. Or she might need to find a professional Christian counselor to talk with about her problems. Whatever the case may be, telling someone else takes the burden off of you. You alone cannot help your friend escape the risky habits she's in bondage to. You are not a counselor, and when you stay quiet as your friend is in danger, you risk her life. The longer she continues the behavior, the more addicted she will become. Don't stay silent. Doing so could cause you to regret it for the rest of your life.

I have a friend who kept her friend's secret. She felt that she should tell someone but just didn't know whom to confide in. She was afraid that if she told someone, she would lose her friend.

So she didn't tell. But guess what? She lost her friend anyway. That friend continued on in her cycle of destruction and eventually ended up dying because of her addiction. Trust me, you don't want to live with that kind of regret. Speak up now before it's too late.

Think about it this way. God may have put you in your friend's life for this very time when she needs help. He may have given her your friendship because he knew that you would do the thing she would need when the time came. Proverbs 27:6 says, "The wounds of a friend are trustworthy." Even though you may feel like you are wounding your friend by asking someone to intervene and help her, you may really

> *She was afraid that if she told someone she would lose her friend. So she didn't tell. But guess what? **She lost her friend anyway.***

saving her life. God could use your involvement to get her attention and to help her step back on the right road.

She may realize that she's been going down a dangerous path and may choose to repent and turn away from her sin. While you can't make that happen in someone else's life, you can offer truth in love when appropriate. One day your friend may thank you for intervening and getting her help. She will realize that you did it to keep her from destroying her life. In the meantime, pray that she will turn back to God and choose repentance and restoration. You may want to claim the above verse for your friend as you pray that God will turn her life around.✱

1. Have you ever found out something about a friend that caused you to worry for her safety? If so, what did you do?

2. If your friend has a dangerous habit, which leader or trusted adult can you talk to about the situation? List his or her name here. Now choose a time when you will talk to this person. Write that here.

3. What consequences could your friend, or someone else, suffer if you stay silent about her problem?

4. How do you think your friend will react when she finds out that you confided in someone? Do you think she will eventually understand why you did it and thank you someday?

We Asked... You Told:
your comments about...
FRIENDS

survey question: **What qualities do you look for in a friend?**

I like when friends are trustworthy and real, like when they can be themselves around you. —Kristen, 14

Someone who makes me laugh until my abs hurt and a Christian who can help me be accountable. —Brittany, 16

Honesty, loyalty, a good sense of humor, a person I know will always have my back. —Lauren, 15

Nice, loyal, respects elders, doesn't cuss, has manners, funny, and modest. —Michelle, 12

A good friend is honest, patient, compassionate, not quick to judge, and faithful. The list could go on and on, but the most important thing to me in a friend is her heart. Is she reflecting who she really is, or is she just putting on a mask? —Erica, 17

Trustworthy—I can tell them secrets, and they won't tell the whole world. —Natasha, 13

The qualities I look for in a friend are understanding, forgiving, honesty, and competitiveness. I would like to have a competitive friend because it makes things a lot more fun! —Kathryn, 13

She needs to be trustworthy, funny, a good student, and godly. —Stevie, 15

Someone who I know loves the Lord so that when I ask her for advice she will look to God and not just give me her opinion. —Samantha, 16

Someone who has the same values I do. It's nice if she's funny and a good shopper as well! —Lindsay, 15

My friends are loyal, sweet, funny, and silly! Most of us love doing girly things like watching Disney movies or chick flicks, shopping, or just talking. My closest friends are Christians, but I have some friends who aren't. —Jana Caitlin, 15

A Christian who is truthful and supportive and who will hold me accountable. Someone who is there for you no matter what. —Hannah, 14

The qualities I look for in a friend are the qualities that I hear about Jesus—loyal, trustworthy, genuine, loving, compassionate, and overall just a pleasant person to be around. —Nicole, 15

I think a friend should be someone who not only loves you but is completely devoted to Jesus Christ. I want my friend to be someone that I can lean on when temptation, trials, and worldly things become overwhelming. —Jessie, 14

I want a friend who is going to be a good influence, is sweet and will lead me down the right path with God. I've always found that the best girlfriends I've ever had are always in my youth group. Godly girls seem to be better friends, virtuous and unselfish in their ways. —Sarah, 14

My best friend and I can read each other like a book, and sometimes we don't even need words. LOL! —Nicole, 14

A true friend never puts you down or turns her back on you. She should also support you and help you get through hard times. —Vanessa, 17

Dedication. I don't like it when a good friend flip-flops to other girls who are more popular or just hangs out with them so they will get more attention from the guys. —Kaitlyn, 13

I want friends that would never pressure me into a situation that I don't want to be in! —Victoria, 13

I like a friend who doesn't care what other people think. It would also be nice if we can pray together. —Emily, 14

I look for people who are sincere, caring, joyful, honest, and passionate about Christ. A good friend will never let a guy come between us. A good friend is also someone who sincerely lifts you up. —Taylor, 15

I look for honesty, loyalty, and a sense of humor. I also look for those who are followers of Christ and are headed the same direction spiritually as I am. —Lauren, 16

I look for a good Christian who is nice, doesn't lie to me, is up-front, honest, trustworthy, loyal, and will stand up for me if people are talking about me! —Kirstie, 14

I look for some one who doesn't do what other kids are doing these days— drinking, partying, smoking, etc. I look for someone who shares the same interests as me. —Laura, 14

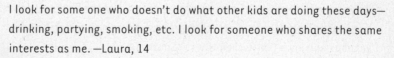

I look for someone who is fun and loves God, but most of all, someone I can just be me with. I want a friend I don't have to hide things from or pretend to be someone I'm not. —Brooke, 13

I look for someone who is willing to be open and honest, someone who looks beyond stereotypes and does not hide behind a mask. —Kendra, 16 ✳

good news is worth sharing, right?

by Whitney Prosperi

Picture this. Your best friend finds out that Mr. Tall, Dark and Handsome has a huge crush on you. He has been totally infatuated since the beginning of the school year. He doesn't think you would be interested, so he goes to your friend instead of you. Your friend knows that you have always kind of had a secret thing for him but never thought he was interested. Now that she's learned this new info, she has the power to get you two together. Great news, huh? Here's the catch—she never mentions it to you. Not once.

What does this situation teach you about your friend? It shows you that she's not really a friend at all. Real friends share good news. They would never keep something great like that to themselves. Now you probably have guessed where I'm going with this. Sharing good news. If you are a believer, you have the best news anyone could ever have. You know the way to receive heaven and eternal life. You understand how someone can escape living out forever in hell. Forever. You know how to have peace in this world, which is filled to the brim with chaos and pain. You have a personal relationship with Jesus Christ. What does that say about you if you don't share it with your friends?

Maybe you are all about sharing your faith. Your friends know where you stand, and you have told them how to become a Christian. But if you are like the rest of us who sometimes have a hard time opening our mouths to witness, the following words may give you some practical help.

Be yourself. God doesn't want you to morph into Billy Graham overnight and start holding church services in your school auditorium. He wants to use you in the circle of influence where he's placed you. Acts 17:26 says, "From one man He has made every nation of men to live all over the earth and has determined their appointed times and the boundaries of where they live." You are a part of your generation for a reason. You are in your school, your extra-curricular activities, and your group of friends so that they can hear about him. He wants to use you with the personality he has put in you to reach others. The question isn't, can he use you? It's, will you let him do it?

Pray. Ask God to place a burden on your heart for those you know that don't have a relationship with him. Ask him to help you see them as he sees them. You might make a "Top 5" list of friends and put it somewhere you can see it every day. Maybe you'll place it on your mirror or in your Bible, and when you see it, you'll be reminded to pray for them. Ask God to soften their hearts to hear the truth and to open doors for you to share.

Be ready. Have you ever been in a situation where you knew God opened a door for you to share about him and you just sat there trying to figure out what to say? I've been there so many times I don't even want to count. If you have too, don't beat yourself up. Instead, make sure you're ready next time. How? By staying in contact with God and by keeping him first in your life. When we're choosing obedience in other areas, witnessing just comes more naturally. First Peter 3:15 says, "But set apart the Messiah as Lord in your hearts, and always be ready to give a defense to anyone who asks you for a reason for the hope that is in you."

Speak up. This may seem like the scariest part, but honestly it's just intimidating until you start talking. Once you open your mouth, you'll find that God gives you the courage matched with the words to say. You don't have to know all the answers. No one does, not even preachers. Just share what God has done in your life. This is often called your testimony. It's simply telling about the difference Jesus has made in you. It's also a good idea to learn some Bible verses so you can share what God says. A great place to start is John 3:16, which says, "For God loved the world in this way: He gave His One and Only Son, so that everyone who believes in Him will not perish but have eternal life." You may want to write out a few verses and put them in your Bible or backpack so you can get to them if you need them in a witnessing situation. You may also want to take a class at your church or read a book about how to be an effective witness. The more prepared you are ahead of time, the easier it will be for you to open your mouth when faced with a witnessing opportunity.

> Speak up. This may seem like the scariest part, but honestly it's just intimidating until you start talking.

Trust that God is the One who changes hearts. While God calls you and me to share the truth, we cannot make someone believe no matter what we say. You may have studied hundreds of Bible verses or prayed for months, but God is the only One who can completely change the human heart. Practice patience. Often when we witness, it's just the first step in someone coming to know Christ. The Bible uses the illustration of planting a seed. After you plant the truth about Jesus, it may take a while for the seed to spring up. But that doesn't mean it's not growing. One day you may have the privilege of introducing that friend to Jesus. Wow! That's the greatest thing a friend can do.

Take a minute to ask yourself: *What kind of friend am I?* Do you have the most incredible news that you could share with someone about how to find peace, security, and eternal life, and you haven't shared that? Or are you the kind of friend who will share what you know, even though it means you may risk feeling uncomfortable at times? Go ahead. Be a real friend. Eternity is closer than you think. ✳

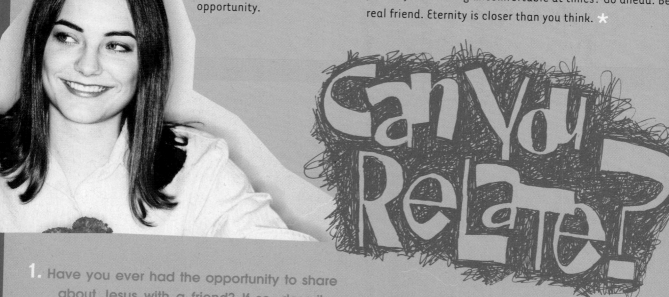

Can you Relate?

1. Have you ever had the opportunity to share about Jesus with a friend? If so, describe what happened.

2. On a scale of one to ten, with ten being the best, how often do you take opportunities to share about Christ with your friends?

3. Write down some of the things you are involved with. How can you be a witness in those different areas of your life?

4. List five people you know who don't have a personal relationship with Jesus. How will you remember to pray for these people every day?

5. What are some things you can do to be prepared ahead of time for when a witnessing situation arises?

your relationship with... Family

me?
a trendsetter?

by Whitney Prosperi

Do you remember when you were in fifth grade? You probably idolized the sixth graders. And when you were in sixth, you probably loved to copy the older students. If you're like most girls, you've always watched with great interest the girls who were older than you. You wanted to talk like, dress like, look like and act like these girls who seem so much more confident and independent. Whether we know it or not, we're always looking for role models to pattern our lives after. In fact, you could probably list five or ten girls off the top of your head that you have watched and wanted to be like.

But here's a question. Have you ever thought of yourself as a role model? If you have a younger sister, brother, or cousin, you are an example. And even if you don't have any younger relatives, you can bet someone is watching you. There may be a neighbor or girl who attends your church who looks up to you. She wants to act just like you. She listens as you talk to your friends and notices the choices you make. Think about that for a minute. If a younger girl decides to imitate you, what kind of person will she become? Kind of scary, isn't it? We never think of ourselves as the ones setting the trends, but in many ways we are.

If you're an older sister, you have the opportunity to lead the way in your family. God calls you to be an example to your younger siblings. Will you take the role of a mentor, living out a lifestyle of love and purity in your family? Will you set a positive example in the choices you make? You may not believe it, but your younger siblings watch everything you do, and they will copy you someday. Make sure that as they are following you, you are following Jesus.

First Timothy 4:12 urges us, "No one should despise your youth; instead, you should be an example to the believers in speech, in conduct, in love, in faith, in purity." It seems that our culture encourages us to throw caution to the wind, with the excuse of being young. But God expects more from us. Rather than waste the gift of youth, why not use it as a powerful influence? Many of the people who have literally changed the world have been young. Consider the possibility that you might be one of them. Your example may change someone else's life or influence a whole nation.

Think back over the last forty-eight hours. How would your actions measure up against the verse above? If someone was watching you, what kind of example would they have heard in the words you chose? Were you mean or critical? Did you pass along a juicy piece of gossip? How about your conduct? If a parent, teacher, or youth leader were to "grade" your conduct and actions, what would you receive? Have your actions demonstrated love? This may be the hardest place of all to set an example.

> **If a younger girl decides to imitate you, what kind of person will she become? Kind of scary, isn't it? We never think of ourselves as the ones setting the trends, but in many ways we are.**

If you have younger brothers and sisters, your patience may be pushed to the max. It's so easy to act mean or just ignore them. Maybe you need to apologize to someone in your family for something you said or did. If so, make sure you do that before you lay your head on your pillow tonight.

While it's great to be a positive example in the way you live and the choices you make, the best role models offer a heritage of faith. Do you take opportunities to encourage those younger than you to

"But whoever causes the downfall of one of these little ones who believe in Me—it would be better for him if a heavy millstone were hung around his neck and he were thrown into the sea." Mark 9:42

commit their lives to Christ? Do you pa along what you've learned? Have you ev shared how to become a Christian with som one in your family or your neighborhood?

A friend of mine became a Christian wh she was about ten years old. She tells t story of how she constantly left Bible vers in her little sister's room and told her abo Jesus every day. She taught her songs a Bible stories so that her little sister wou understand what it meant to follow Jesu And one day she had the opportunity to pr with her sister as she committed her life Christ. Instead of taking her little sister f granted, she chose the irreplaceable role encourager and example.

Will you leave a legacy of purity to t girls who are coming behind you? If you dor want your younger cousin pushing the limi with her boyfriend when she's older, then mak sure you model a life of purity now. Guard th messages you put in your mind through T movies, music, and the Internet. Decide th you'll set personal boundaries now, and the commit to live by them day by day.

Remember the warning of Jesus to those who would tempt someone younger or weaker to sin. "But whoever causes the downfall of one of these little ones who believe in Me—it would be better for him if a heavy millstone were hung around his neck and he were thrown into the sea" (Mark 9:42). Do you take your position of role model as seriously as God takes it? If not, stop right now and say a prayer asking him to help you as you set some trends—the kind that make a lasting impact. ✴

Can You Relate?

1. Who is someone that you have looked up to as a role model? What qualities does she have that you admire?

2. Think of your realm of influence. Now take a minute to list some younger girls that may be watching you. Remember, you may not know them personally. They might just be looking on from a distance.

3. What are some things you could do to point these younger girls to Jesus?

4. How can you be a role model to your younger brothers, sisters, and cousins?

5. Because you are a role model, is there an action or attitude in your life that you should allow God to change? If so, how will you cooperate with him to do that?

What Kind of Role

start!

You tell others about God's blessings

every chance you get

only when they sneeze

When it comes to purity, you think of

bottled water

Your sister or brother would say you are nice

most of the time

Your friends would describe you as

sometimes

flaky

loyal

Your motto is

"others first"

When you overhear some juicy gossip, you

"numero uno"

pass it on to a few on your buddy list

QUIZ:

STOP, DROP, AND "ROLE"—Your character is going up in flames. If you want to redeem your reputation refocus your attention on being a God-pleaser rather than a people pleaser. "Happy are those who keep His decrees and seek Him with all their heart" (Psalms 119:2).

by Julie Shannan

Model Are You?

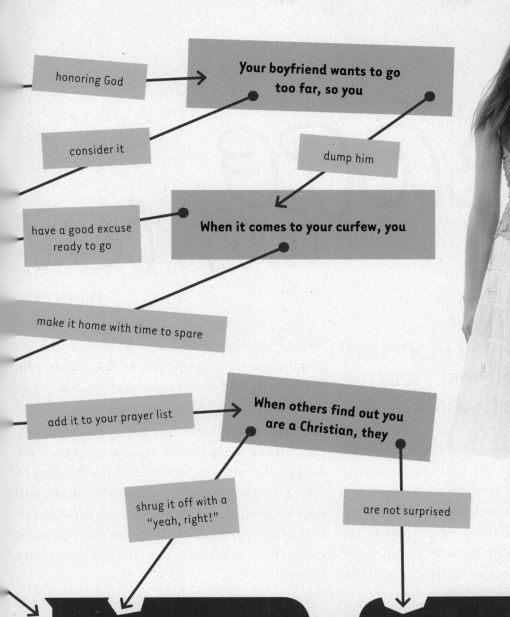

honoring God → **Your boyfriend wants to go too far, so you**

consider it

dump him

have a good excuse ready to go

When it comes to your curfew, you

make it home with time to spare

add it to your prayer list → **When others find out you are a Christian, they**

shrug it off with a "yeah, right!"

are not surprised

"ROLE" UP YOUR SLEEVES—
You have some work to do, but it's worth the sweat. People are watching, so don't miss opportunities to reflect your faith positively on others. "Live your life in a manner worthy of the gospel of Christ" (Philippians 1:27).

YOU'RE ON A "ROLE"—
Congratulations, you're on the right path. Keep your focus on God, and let your life be an example for others to follow. "In the same way, let your light shine before men, so that they may see your good works and give glory to your Father in heaven" (Matthew 5:16).

THE ESCAPE ARTIST

by Susie Davis

A guy in my senior class pulled off the most creative escape from school ever.

We were all sitting in English class discussing a novel, and this guy John was especially rowdy. He just wouldn't keep quiet. He kept making smarty remarks to our otherwise patient teacher. When she could bear no more, she looked at him and said tersely, "John, you need to excuse yourself to the study closet and stay there until the end of class." (The study closet was located in our English room but it was self-contained with its own door.)

Upon the teacher's request, John strode to the study closet, walked in, and closed the door. And all became quiet. Unusually quiet. After about twenty minutes, my teacher decided to invite John back to class, thinking perhaps he had learned his lesson. She walked to the study closet, opened the door, and gasped loudly yelling, "John!"

We had no idea what had happened, so we all raced to the study closet and realized quickly why our teacher had reacted so violently. John was gone.

There was no other door out of the closet, and there was no window either. It looked as if John had disappeared into thin air. We did a quick search of the classroom and found nothing. My teacher was close to absolute panic, her feet still glued to the spot where she discovered he was missing, when suddenly she said aloud, "John escaped through the ceiling."

Apparently there was more than one way out of the room, and John had discovered it. He popped out the ceiling tile and pulled himself through into the crawl space above the room where he found an opening on to the roof and shimmied down a tree to freedom, at least for a while.

I don't know exactly what happened to John after they found him and hauled him into the principal's office although I know he got in a lot of trouble.

And while you've got to hand it to him for escaping the immediate punishment of having to sit in the study closet, he didn't escape punishment altogether. And he certainly didn't escape the people who were in authority over him: the teacher, the principal, and his parents. In fact, he got in worse trouble for running away from those people. Not too smart if you think it through.

> IT'S ABOUT A REBELLIOUS ATTITUDE TOWARDS THOSE IN AUTHORITY AND WE ALL STRUGGLE WITH IT.

Honestly, the smartest thing would have been for John to calm down and get quiet. If he had done that when asked, then he wouldn't have had to sit in the study closet alone, and he wouldn't have felt the need to escape, and he wouldn't have ended up in so much trouble. But that is not the way it played out, and I think there is an explanation for that type of response. It's about a rebellious attitude toward those in authority, and we all struggle with it. Frankly, it started a long time ago.

In the book of Genesis there is a story of a couple who were determined to resist authority. They too felt deprived because they were required to abide by the rules. They wanted some freedom and autonomy. So they jumped out there past the mandated guidelines and ended up just like my friend John, trying to outrun

the consequences of rebellious actions and outrun those in charge. Their names? Adam and Eve. And their first thought when they were in trouble with authority? Run. Hide. Escape.

Let's start with some history. God, in the book of Genesis, created an unbelievable garden for Adam and Eve. They had no rules but one. And Eve knew it well. She even knew the rule by heart and stated,

> "THEN THE MAN AND HIS WIFE HEARD THE SOUND OF THE LORD GOD WALKING IN THE GARDEN AT THE TIME OF THE EVENING BREEZE, AND THEY HID THEMSELVES FROM THE LORD GOD AMONG THE TREES OF THE GARDEN. SO THE LORD GOD CALLED OUT TO THE MAN AND SAID TO HIM, "WHERE ARE YOU?"
> GENESIS 3:8–9

"But about the fruit of the tree in the middle of the garden, God said, 'You must not eat it or touch it, or you will die'" (Genesis 3:3). But knowing that rule by heart

did not stop her from eating the fruit. The fruit was appealing (breaking the rules can appear appealing), and she took the bite, munching deep into the fruit. And believe it or not, she invited her husband Adam to eat along with her—much better to take someone along with you than get in trouble alone. So they both made a decision and crossed the line. They broke the rules established by God. In other words, they sinned.

Unfortunately, sin is not without consequence. Though we'd like to think that we can get away with sin, the consequences of sin trail along after us. And one of those consequences is that it wrecks our relationship with those in authority. It creates alienation; it often makes us want to run away from the people we disobey.

Just take a look at what happens after Adam and Eve made the decision to bite into the very thing that God directly prohibited.

"Then the man and his wife heard the sound of the LORD God walking in the garden at the time of the evening breeze, and they hid themselves from the LORD God among the trees of the garden. So the

LORD God called out to the man and said to him, 'Where are you?'" (Genesis 3:8–9).

See what they did? They hid. *The truth is that when we make decisions to disobey those in authority, it is a natural impulse to feel like running to escape the inevitable consequence.* Adam and Eve knew that there was a problem. The minute they made the choice to disobey, they recognized their sin, and then they ran. They ran to find a place to hide, fearful of authority. They huddled together in the garden, and when they heard God coming, they ducked behind a tree.

Just imagine the scene. There are Adam and Eve hiding behind the trees, and there is God asking, "Where are you?" Do you honestly think God couldn't find them? God could see them. And so this scene plays out more like a father playing hide-n-seek with a toddler. The dad counts to ten while the toddler runs to hide. And the toddler, not savvy enough to hide well, goes for the couch and pulls a blanket over her head. She attempts to lie still but is breathing heavily and wiggling like crazy. And her dad is asking (while looking at the lumpy, moving form on the couch), "Where are you?"

So I have a question for you. *When you disobey the rules and then you are faced with the inevitable issues that come when dealing with the people in authority over you, where are you?* Are you like Adam and Eve (and my classmate John), running to escape the consequences? What is your usual reaction?

While running might be the impulse, it's not really the best option. And while we might like to rationalize our actions or debate the validity of the rules,

THERE WILL ALWAYS BE PEOPLE OVER US, COMPELLING US TO OBEY.

that's not really going to be the best idea either. *Like it or not, there are always going to be rules. There will always be people over us, compelling us to obey. And that is because we are all under authority. Every single one of us. And we will be for the rest of our lives.* As much as we would like to think that one day we could be free from anyone having any say in our lives, we will always have someone that is in authority over us. Teachers, parents, policemen, bosses, presidents—there will always be someone.

So the Bible has some practical advice for those of us under authority. *Romans 13:1–3 states, "Everyone must submit to the governing authorities, for there is no authority except from God, and those that exist are instituted by God. So then, the one who resists the authority is opposing God's command, and those who oppose it will bring judgment on themselves. For rulers are not a terror to good conduct, but to bad. Do you want to be unafraid of the authority? Do good and you will have its approval."*

The Bible has offered some practical advice for dealing with this issue. Basically, resisting authority will bring judgment, and submitting to authority will win approval. That is what the Bible promises. While doing your own thing, even when it's against the rules, may make you feel independent and free, on the other side of that freedom is judgment, which isn't so much fun. And while submitting to authority sometimes seems demeaning and humbling, the promise of approval is actually nice.

So you really have two choices when it comes to dealing with authority. Submit or resist. And while we could debate endlessly on how valid the rules are, **there really is only one valid question: Where are you?**

Can You Relate?

1. List the people in your life who are in authority over you.

2. What is your first response when someone asks you to do something you don't want to do? Why?

3. Why does breaking the rules sometimes look so appealing?

4. How can you develop a submissive and respectful attitude toward those in authority over you?

5. Have you ever been an "escape artist," trying to outrun the consequences of disobedience? What was the eventual result of running?

6. How might approval (by doing the right thing) from those in authority over you make your life happier?

7. Romans 3 states that "resisting authority is opposing God's command." Have you considered that rebelling against those in authority over you is actually opposing God himself?

8. Is there ever a time when it is appropriate or acceptable to oppose authority? Are there specific biblical guidelines to follow when doing so?

SIBS DRIVING YOU CRAZY?

by Whitney Prosperi

Have you ever let your brother or sister get in trouble for something you did, all the while keeping your mouth shut so you wouldn't receive punishment? I have, and I can't say I'm proud of it. When I was five years old or so, my younger brother and I were playing in the new house my parents were having built. In order to save money, my mom and dad were doing a lot of the painting themselves. My brother and I were playing in one of the rooms they had just painted the whitest white you have ever seen. It looked perfect, and we were instructed not to touch the walls—and not even to breathe in their direction.

Enter the can of orange soda. I should have known better. Those cans always explode and spurt out when you don't want them to—like on a newly painted white wall. You guessed it. I opened it. It would be more accurate to say that an atomic bomb of orange exploded all over the perfect white walls. What do you think we did? Ran to tell our parents what happened so they could correct the problem before it became permanent? Of course not. We weren't that levelheaded. We ran into another room and played there until later that night. A psychiatrist might call that living in denial.

Later when my parents saw the walls and had an explosion of their own, I wimped out on telling them the truth. They asked my younger brother what happened, and he told them I spilled the soda. Then they asked me. You guessed it. I lied. I told them he did it. I bet you're thinking right about now how glad you are that I'm not your older sister. Because I was the oldest, my parents assumed that I was telling the truth, and they punished my little brother. Honestly, I don't think he remembers the whole event because he was too young when it happened. But I definitely remember. And it makes me feel sad each time I do.

> As Christians we are called to love and serve our families. If we can't even show his love to someone who lives under the same roof as us, how can we love the rest of the world?

You probably have your own story of a time when you [ac]ted less than loving to a brother or sister. It's so easy [to] do. They are around ALL the time, so we are tempted [to] take them for granted. Maybe your brother or sister is [yo]unger and constantly follows you around. Or they might [no]t respect your space and personal things. Let's face [it]: being kind to our brothers and sisters can sometimes [b]e a challenge.

But did you know that as Christians we are called to [l]ove and serve our families? If we can't even show his love [t]o someone who lives under the same roof as us, how can we [l]ove the rest of the world? If you want a true test of your faith, [j]ust look at how you treat your family. We may find it easy to put on our spiritual face at youth group, but it's impossible to fake it at home. What does how you treat your brothers and sisters reveal about your heart?

Friends will come and go, but our families will be around for the rest of our lives. That's why it's important to keep the big picture in mind when dealing with your siblings. If your sister does something that drives you crazy, like borrowing your shoes or exaggerating stories, try to think forward five years—or fifteen. Do you want to let a small, irritating behavior drive a wedge between the two of you? Absolutely not. Then decide to offer grace and forgiveness for the things she does that bug you. It will be the glue that seals your relationship over the course of your lives.

We all know the children's rhyme, "Sticks and stones may break my bones, but words will never hurt me." While that little saying has been passed down for several generations, it really isn't true at all. Words can hurt more than anything. And girls especially have the knack for knowing the thing to say that will hurt the worst. It's not something to brag about.

I have a friend who has told me how much she regrets the way she talked to her sisters growing up. She said that she just fired off whatever rude comment she wanted to without thinking of the long-term consequences. This friend says that she is actually still repairing the damage in those relationships twenty years later.

How about you? What kind of words fly out of your mouth when you're talking to your brothers and sisters? Do you regularly tell them they are stupid or put them down in other ways? Do you make fun of them or just plain ignore them? If so, remember that these words will make an impact on them forever. You may need to put a filter on that mouth of yours before it does any more damage. Ephesians 4:29 says, "No rotten talk should come from your mouth, but only what is good for the building up of someone in need, in order to give grace to those who hear." I once heard someone say that before she says

anything she asks herself: "Is this true? Is it kind? Is it useful?" If we ran every word through that filter, things would be a lot quieter around our houses—and so much more peaceful.

> Did you know that God put you in your exact family for a reason? God may just want to use you today to make a brother or sister's life easier. What can you do to lighten his or her load?

You may have never given it much thought before, but did you know that God put you in your exact family for a reason? He chose your parents and your brothers and sisters. The fact that these people are in your life is not an accident. Think about it for a minute. He may just want to use you today to make a brother or sister's life easier. What can you do to lighten his or her load? Maybe they struggle with a certain subject in school that you are particularly good at and could help them in. Or they might need some advice about a difficult friend situation they're experiencing. Maybe they just need to know you'll listen and support them. Why not change your focus from you to them? Take your eyes off of what they do that bugs you and place it on how you can help and serve them. You'll be amazed at how your attitude will change. ★

1. Think back over the last week. Does the way you treated your brother or sister show that you are a Christian? Explain your answer.

2. Is there an action that your brother or sister does that drives you crazy? If so, how can you deal with them in a loving way rather than exploding?

3. What does the way you talk to your siblings reveal about your heart? Is there a change you need to make? If so, how will you go about doing that?

4. Do you need to forgive your sibling for something? If so, make the decision to do that today.

5. Is there something for which you need to ask forgiveness from a sister or brother? If your answer is yes, when will you go to them and make that right?

Wigged Out

by Susie Davis

With a roll of my eyes, I grudgingly grabbed my keys off the kitchen counter and walked toward the garage. My mother had given me the assignment to drive my grandmother to the local beauty center to buy her a new wig. My grandma had just moved in with our family while she was going through chemotherapy treatments for cancer. The chemo had caused her hair to thin substantially and she wore wigs to cover her balding head.

I didn't know why I should have to run this errand with my grandma when my mom would be much better at it. And besides, didn't my mom care that I had made after school plans with my friends? Didn't she know that I was loaded up with homework? Didn't she know that a sixteen year old, busy with high school activities, just didn't have time to drive her grandmother all the way across town to look at wigs?

As we got in the car, I quickly turned up my music hoping at least to enjoy the trip and just as quickly my grandma started asking me about school.

"How is high school going for you, sweetie?"

"Fine," I replied.

"Do you like your classes?"

"Yes," I mumbled.

"Are you still dating that nice boy?"

"Uh-huh," I stammered.

And with the conversation going nowhere fast, she quietly hummed and looked out the window.

By the time we arrived at the beauty center, I was really hoping for some quick decision making on her part. From what I could tell by looking at my watch, if she decided on a wig fast, I could meet up with my friends and move forward with my plans.

But my grandmother took her time, looking at this wig and that, asking my opinion about the style and color. I was growing more and more impatient.

Finally, a saleswoman came over to help her make a decision. After trying on several, she carefully fitted my grandmother in the wig of her choice, and the purchase was complete. My grandmother was happy and I was relieved.

As we started the trip home, I decided that speeding things up a little in the car would get us there sooner. I noticed my grandmother tightening her grip on the seat as I sped along. Finally when she could no longer stand it, she asked me to slow down; and just as I was about to defend my driving, I took a corner too sharply and nudged into a tree.

I got out of the car, checked the bumper and was relieved that there was no damage to the tree or the car. Then I got back in, apologized to my grandma, and drove carefully home.

The incident shook me up. Nearly wrecking your car at sixteen should I suppose. But the thing that bothered me most was that I was so impatient. So selfish. So uncaring. And so wigged out about a small change in my schedule. *My* schedule and my fun overruled everything else in *my* life, including my grandmother.

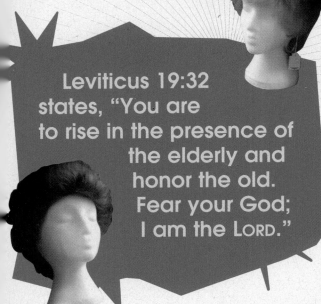

Leviticus 19:32 states, "You are to rise in the presence of the elderly and honor the old. Fear your God; I am the LORD."

The Bible has some things to say about honoring our elders. Leviticus 19:32 states, "You are to rise in the presence of the elderly and honor the old. Fear your God; I am the LORD." Honestly, I wasn't honoring my grandmother with the way I was acting. To honor someone is to esteem and respect them. To assign value or worth. When we give someone value, we are interested in pleasing them and placing their needs before our own. In my situation I was doing neither with my grandmother and therefore, not only was I dishonoring her, I was dishonoring God.

Some years later my grandma did eventually die of cancer. I'll never forget the phone call I got while I was away at college. My dad called late one night to tell me that she had slipped into a coma and that the doctor's final prognosis was grim. I was so upset about the call that I borrowed a friend's car and sped home, crying all the way.

When I finally arrived at the hospital, I quietly walked in to see my grandma. There she was, unable to respond. I tenderly reached for her hand and called her name. No movement.

I stood looking at her, breathing slowly and remembering my time with her. The times we had laughed while playing a card game called Pig. And the times we had enjoyed watching her favorite shows together. I also remembered the times I had squabbles with her, the times I had been impatient and selfish.

In the very next moment, her eyes fluttered, a[nd] I felt her fingers lightly lift and touch my hand.

I leaned forward and hugged her frail body [as] gently as I could. She had spoken in the only wa[y] she could, reassuring me that she forgave me a[nd] that she loved me.

Then I silently prayed. I prayed that God would forgive my terse moments with my grandma. I prayed that he would forgive my impatience and my lack of concern. I prayed that she would know that I loved her. And then, through tears, I spoke to her.

"Grandma, I love you. I am so sad that you are in so much pain. Thank you for being such a great grandma. I also want you to know how sorry I am for not honoring you in all the ways I should. Please, forgive me. Please let me know that you forgive me and you love me."

I prayed that God would forgive my terse moments with my grandma. I prayed that He would forgive my impatience and my lack of concern. I prayed that she would know that I loved her.

Sometimes it is hard to keep a perspective about the important things in life, but maybe this will provide a perspective to you about your grandparents. It might give you an idea how worthwhile it is to honor and love your elders.

Don't get wigged out, thinking only of yourself like I did the day my grandma needed a little help, because you might live to regret that kind of behavior. Instead, think of ways to esteem those people in your life by putting their needs in front of your own. Whether it is driving them on an errand or listening to their stories, fit some time into your day to care for them in a way that will show that you love and value them and in that way you will honor God. ✱

Can You Relate?

1. Who are the elders in your life? List three to five people who you would consider people who fit the description of elders.

2. Think about any interactions you have had with them in the last month. Have you demonstrated respect for them?

3. What one thing could you do for someone who is older than you to show that you respect him or her?

4. I regretted that I was so impatient with my grandmother, and I almost didn't get a chance to make things right with her. Is there someone in your life who needs to hear an apology from you?

5. What are some creative ways you could seek forgiveness and build a bridge of respect with them?

6. Pray for the wisdom and courage to make things right with the elders in your life.

GET HELP NOW!

by Whitney Prosperi

Family secrets. It might seem that every family has them. For some it's just that Grandpa snores like a lion or that Mom isn't really a blonde. But for others family secrets are painful realities covered under layers of lies. Maybe you know what I'm talking about. You have held a secret so horrible and shameful that you felt you couldn't tell anyone. It's just become a part of who you are, and you feel that it will never change.

Abuse is like that. It cripples someone so much that she finds it hard to reach out for help. It's easier to stay in the situation than to risk retaliation for exposing a family secret. Abuse comes in all forms, and it takes place in all kinds of families. You can't tell which families hold the secret just by looking at them or listening to their conversations. It affects all races, all neighborhoods, and all religions. And it's more common than most people think it is.

Many suffer from physical abuse from parents or siblings who find it hard to control their tempers. We're talking more than discipline here. This borders on violence that results in bruises and cuts. For some it may mean burns or other forms of cruelty. Maybe you cover these bruises with long sleeves or claim that you are a klutz, but inside you want to tell others the truth about what is happening to you. You know that you are in danger if you stay in your current situation, but you may not know where to turn for help.

Others suffer silently under attacks of constant verbal abuse. If this is your situation, someone in your family continuously demoralizes you and cuts you down. Once again, this goes way beyond discipline. It's the never-ending onslaught of hateful and cruel words. You may have gotten so used

this kind of talk that you see it as normal, but deep down you know that it's a subtle type of abuse that destroys your soul and mind. You feel that it's slowly destroying you from the inside out.

Another kind of abuse is sexual abuse. One out of every three girls has experienced this violation, and the numbers grow each year. If this is you, you know who you are. And you have worn this shame like a heavy coat that weighs you down. The abuse may have come from a cousin, your uncle, your father, or someone else in your life. Maybe he has threatened you that if you tell he will seriously hurt you or someone you love. You feel trapped like a helpless bird being hunted. You think you have no way out!

But you do. There are people who can help you and who will make sure the abuse you are experiencing will stop for good. You just have to take the first step to expose the situation. Will you choose one person with whom you can confide your secret? Maybe as you read

Abuse comes in all forms, and it takes place in all kinds of families. You can't tell which families hold the secret just by looking at them or listening to their conversations.

these words, you thought of a youth leader, teacher, or minister that you would feel safe talking with. If so, call or e-mail him or her today and ask to meet sometime in the next day or so to talk. And don't let fear keep you from following through on your conversation. It will probably be one of the hardest things you ever do, but it will be one of the best choices you'll make in

When you tell someone about your situation, you're taking the very first step to becoming whole.

When you tell someone about your situation, you're taking the very first step to becoming whole.

Secrets have the capacity to paralyze us. But when we share them with someone else, it's like we're opening a door for healing to begin. When you tell someone about your situation, you're taking the first step to becoming whole. You will begin to understand that you're not alone in the journey to healing. Others will be able to help you, some who have experienced the same pain you

life. Tell this person the truth and trust that he or she will help you. And if for some reason the person you've chosen doesn't "hear" you or believe you, find someone who does. There will be someone out there who can help you. Don't give up on finding him or her.

have and others who simply want to offer tangible hope and assistance. They'll help you understand that the abuse wasn't your fault. Even though you may have felt like it was, you were simply the victim of someone else's sin. You are not responsible for their behavior. When you do confide in someone, you will want to ask him or her to find you a Christian counselor who will walk with you through the process of healing.

While the tendency is to hold the secret of abuse so close that we never tell another soul, God will give us the strength and courage to speak the truth. Will you ask him to help you get help? He will. Ask him today. **Psalm 10:14 says, "But You Yourself have seen trouble and grief, observing it in order to take the matter into Your hands. The helpless entrusts himself to You; You are a helper of the fatherless."**

Know that God cares about your situation and loves you very much. He will use the people that you tell to support and love you. He will heal your wounds no matter how deep they seem to go. While healing is a process and it won't happen overnight, know that God can and will do it. In fact, he's the only one who is able. Healing the brokenhearted is his specialty. Restoring hope is right up his alley. He is a loving Father, full of compassion and mercy. Do you trust him to help you deal with this situation? If so, take the first step and talk to someone today.

"He heals the brokenhearted and binds up their wounds. He counts the number of the stars; He gives names to all of them. Our Lord is great, vast in power; His understanding is infinite" (Psalm 147:3–5). ★

Can You Relate?

1. Have you been forced to keep a secret? If so, how do you feel?

2. What is the scariest part about telling someone what has happened to you? How do you think God will help you overcome your fear?

3. Now imagine that you are out of your current abusive situation and in a safe environment. Describe how you would feel.

4. List some people you trust to whom you could tell your secret.

5. Now pick a time when you will talk to one of the people on your list. Write that here. The sooner you get your secret out in the open, the faster you'll find the help you need. Take that first step as soon as possible.

5 TIPS TO BEING AN AWARD-WINNING DAUGHTER

by Vicki Courtney and Julie Shannan

Have you ever seen those blue ribbons with "World's Best Mom" or "World's Best Dad" on them Cheesy as they are, most parents would be proud to receive one. Being a parent is hard wor and sometimes a thankless job. As a daughter, you can make mom and dad's job easier. Try the five tip below, and, who knows, your efforts may earn you one of those nifty "World's Best Daughter" blue ribbon to hang proudly in your locker—yeah, right!

Try not to zone out when your parents start talking.

Tip #1: Show Them Respect

Show them respect. Sometimes it's hard to understand your parent's point of view, especially if it doesn't line up with yours. Try not to zone out when your parents start talking, but make an effort to listen carefully to their point. If you don't agree, try not to get

fensive. You've probably figured out by now that it
ly makes matters worse. I know it's hard, but take a
w minutes to think about their perspective. Sometimes
en you don't see eye to eye, you have to "agree to dis-
ree." Of course, your parents hold the final say, and you
st respect their rules and boundaries. And remember,
simple "yes ma'am" or "no sir" can do wonders for your
lationship.

Tip #2: TALK TO THEM

Talk to them. "How was your day?" "Fine." "Do you
ave a lot of homework?" "No." "Are you ready for your
iology test tomorrow?" "Sort of." I know it's hard when

Believe it or not, their questions are not
an attempt to annoy you—they just
want to get into your world.

your parents start drilling you with a bunch of questions,
but look at the positive side: At least they care enough to
ask! Try answering with more than one word. Believe it or
not, their questions are not an attempt to annoy you—they
just want to get into your world. Try sharing something
about your day even if they don't initiate the conversation. You might have to get out the smelling salts the first
time you try it; but trust me, a little effort goes a long way.

Tip #3: SAY THANKS EVERY ONCE IN A WHILE

Say thanks every once in awhile. Trips to the m[...] braces, club teams, summer camp, driving on field tri[...] baking cookies for the bake sale, emergency runs to t[...] store for poster board for your project, a college educ[...] tion, and the list goes on and on. A parent's job is nev[...] done. Sometimes it's easy to take it for granted a[...] assume parents owe their kids these things. The truth [...] a lot of kids around the world lack the essentials—a ro[...] over their heads and three square meals a day. Yet mo[...] parents are knocking themselves out to shuttle their ki[...] to countless activities, make it to their games, and sa[...] enough money to get them that iPod Nano for Christma[...] Consider sending your parents an e-mail, leave them [...] note, or just tell them "thanks!" every once in a while.

> A parent's job is never done . . . and sometimes, it's easy to take them for granted.

Tip #4: Cut them some SLACK

Cut them some slack. So Dad mows the lawn in dress socks, loafers, and shorts that are above the knee. Mom can't seem to make it ten minutes without embarrassing you when your friends are over. And bless her heart, the waistband on her jeans comes up to her armpits. As if that's not bad enough, she tucks her shirts in and wears a belt. Yikes! Most parents are not cool, and it's unreasonable to expect them to be someone they're not. I know it's hard to believe, but someday you will likely have kids who think you are highly uncool and laugh when they see your old pictures. Have your mom save those high-waisted jeans for you. You might need them! Ick!

P #5: REMIND THEM THAT THEY ARE LOVED

Remind them that they are loved. A few months ago, I woke up at 5 a.m. to catch an early flight for a speaking engagement. As I was heading down the stairs, I found the greatest surprise from my daughter Paige. She had taped about ten pieces of notebook paper together and written me a sweet note and draped it across the top of the stairs. I was so touched, I cried. I folded that thing up, put it in my bag, and showed it to all my friends. Other times she will leave me a post-it note on my desk or sneak a note into my bag. I have saved every one of them. I would rather have her homemade notes than a store-bought gift any day. Consider leaving your mom or dad a reminder that they are loved. It can be a simple "I love you" on a post-it note, e-mail, or text message. Guaranteed to make your mom cry—or your money back. ✱

Honor your father and mother—which is the first commandment with a promise—that it may go well with you and that you may have a long life in the land.

Ephesians 6:2–3

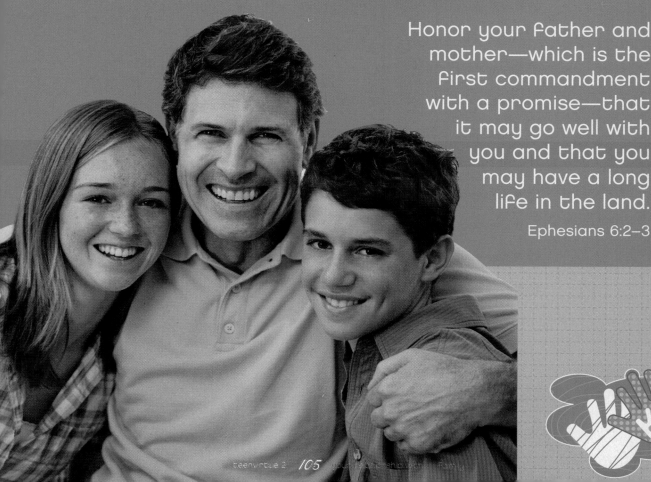

10 Never Evers

1. **Never ever** intentionally take your family for granted.

2. **Never ever** treat your siblings like your worst enemies.

3. **Never ever** forget to tell your parents you love them.

4. **Never ever** assume your parents know that you appreciate all they do for you.

5. **Never ever** forget to call your grandparents once in a while.

6. **Never ever** tell someone in your family that you hate them.

7. **Never ever** assume that you are too young be a spiritual giant in your family.

8. **Never ever** forget that God placed you in your family for a special purpose.

9. **Never ever** speak ill of your family to others.

10. **Never ever** forget that your parents aren't perfect.

We Asked... You TOLD:
your comments about...
YOUR MOM

survey question: **What do you love about your mom?**

My mom is never too busy for me. She leads a hectic life, but she always finds time for me. Whether I'm upset about something, I need help with something, or I just want someone to talk to, she is always there for me. —Paige, 15

I love how my mom is always available when I need to speak with her and offers sound advice. —Kendra, 16

She gives great advice, and she has so much wisdom that she's almost always right! —Deborah, 14

My mom is the most amazing woman on earth! I absolutely love the fact that she is honest with me, and I can be brutally honest with her. It is a total trust thing. —Kaylee, 15

I can talk to her about anything and everything. —Megan, 13

I love how she's always there for me, no matter what, and she believes in me . . . even if no one else does. —Brittany, 15

She is such an extraordinary person. There are so many things that make her special. I guess one thing that really stands out is that she ALWAYS has time for me. Even if she's really busy with work and has five phone calls, she always will make time for me. She really understands me too. I'll tell my friends things, and they might go tell someone else. But when I tell my mom things, I know that she won't tell anyone. —Grace, 12

She is really cool, cooks good food, and she is a good Christian! She is also active at church, and she encourages me to put my faith before anything else! —Kirstie, 14

My mom is honest with me and doesn't try to sugarcoat things. —Lauren, 16

She has the most creative instinct I've ever seen in anyone. Any kind of project, party, team spirit, she's there making up cool stuff. —Kelli, 13

My mom is a really fun, outgoing kind of person. —Taylor, 15

I can talk to her about lots of things, and she is my number one fan! I know that no matter what I have done, she will still love me! —Emily, 14

She's a pretty good judge of character. —Allison, 16

I like how she is always there for me when I need her. She is always volunteering at school and with the youth group on Sunday nights. —Kaitlyn, 13

I love her smile. —Emily, 13

My mom is the best because she listens when I talk to her. She even drives me about forty-five minutes to an hour to ballet classes. —Vanessa, 17

I love how my mom puts others first. She never hesitates to sacrifice something she wants for me or someone in my family. She is such a servant, just like Jesus was. —Rosemary, 14

I love that my mom is always willing to listen. She always has time to hear about the algebra quiz I failed or the boy who broke my heart. —Sarah, 14

I love it that she always knows what to say in a situation. She mentions a Bible verse that I need for that day, or she'll just tell me about her day. It's like we're best friends. —Stephanie, 17

She encourages me to grow in Christ and learn more about him. She is a Sunday school teacher, so she encourages a lot more people than just me! —Linley, 13

I love how my mom is willing to do stuff for me even when I'm not acting my best. I love how she is creative, and she has good ideas for my projects and for making my room look pretty. Most of all, I love how she loves me 100 percent no matter what! —Jana, 15

matter how many times I mess up, she keeps loving me no matter
~~at~~. That's just amazing to me. —Suzanne, 17

She is my best friend! —Breanna, 15

~~e~~ is so selfless and always wants the
~~st~~ for me. —Lindsay, 15

~~ow~~, there are so many things I love about my mom.
She homeschools me so I get to spend a lot of time
with her. I love that she keeps me accountable; that
she is patient, and that she has taught me about God
since I was a baby. —Samantha, 16

~~er~~ servant heart. —Savannah, 13

She is amazingly funny without even trying and very sympathetic as well. —Jennifer, 14

~~he~~ never gives up on people. I love to call her my "supermom." —Marissa, 15

She has confidence in me even when I don't have confidence in myself. —Joanna, 16

She laughs about everything. She is easily amused. —Lacie, 17

She always tells me when I'm good at something, which is nice to hear once in a while. —Kara, 13

She is always there for me with some funny saying of hers that always cheers me up. —Laurel, 15

She somehow always knows when something is wrong and can usually fix it. —Lauren, 15

She never gives up on me. She never stops believing in my dreams,
and she helps me reach my goals. —Kelly, 13

She is encouraging, uplifting, and is a great role
model to me and my friends. —Brittany, 16

My mom is my best friend, and she knows me inside and out,
probably even better than I know myself. —Erica, 17

She is hardworking. Once she's started something, she'll never give up on it,
even though it may be something that seems impossible. —Natasha, 12

My mom knows just the right moment to give me a hug and tell me
she loves me. She's my best friend. —Dayla, 18

I love when my mom and I can spend quality time together and talk like girlfriends. —Nicole, 14 ✱

Dear Dad

by Susie and Will Davis Jr.; Vicki and Keith Courtney

"Listen to your father who gave you life."

Proverbs 23:22a

Dear Dad,

There's this boy, and I really like him. I finally got enough courage to tell him and ask him if he liked me too. It has been a week and still no answer. I have asked him two other times when or if he is going to tell me, and his answer is always "soon." Today at school he promised me that he would write me a note and give it to me after school ended. After school I asked him about it, and he said that he would write a note tonight and give it to me tomorrow. What if he doesn't? Why won't he just tell me? I need answers! Help!

—Jessica, 14

Dear Jessica,

Let me tell you honestly, this guy is not worth your time. He is not valuing you. He is not responding to you as a respectful person would, and so he is not giving you the kind of treatment you deserve.

How would you feel if one of your friends treated you the way he does? Would you keep on hoping she would be nice? I don't think so. You would be steaming mad, and you wouldn't put up with it. But this boy seems to have you stuck in some sort of strange trance. The strange part is his rude behavior and how a

*I*f you will believe me that you can do better and hold on to the fact that there is someone far greater for you, I know you can get over this guy.

girl like you would continue to give him any attention at all. Let him go. I really don't think you should
give him another thought.

You deserve someone who will treat you like the
princess you are, and this guy certainly can't seem to
be that! He's tooling you around. And in response,
you're following around after him. I suggest you forget
about him.

But forgetting him is the hard part, isn't it? You
probably see him in the hall at school every day, and
your friends likely point out where he is at every turn, so
forgetting about him is difficult. But if you will believe
me that you can do better and hold on to the fact that
there is someone far greater for you, I know you can
get over this guy. It sounds like your heart is wrapped
up in his attention, which puts you at a great disadvan-
tage. Honestly, even though its normal for you to be
interested in guys at this age, it would be best for you to
put all that energy and attention into something more
productive for your life—like maybe your friends or your
family or your church youth group, or even a sport or
hobby you really enjoy. Your heart is too young to be
aching and breaking over boys, especially this one.

Love, Dad

Dear Dad,

Do guys REALLY think about sex all the time?

—Eve, 17

Dear Eve,

No, guys don't think about sex all the time. Teenage
boys think about football and lunch and when their math
class will be over. They think about how stupid homework
is, and they think about how infuriating their parents can
be at times. They see the news on TV and wonder about why
things happen in the world, like tsunamis and hurricanes.
They think about God and spiritual things. And they also
think about girls.

They wonder why girls act the way they do and why
girls are seemingly so sensitive compared to boys. And
sometimes they look at girls and see their bodies and yes,
it could lead them to think about sex. Or if a girl walks by
them and she is not especially well covered, it could lead

The trick here is not to let the curiosity and interest lead you to places
that are off limits for this time in your life.

them to think about sex (see "A Thing or Two You Need to
Know about Guys").

Boys are curious about sex just as girls are curious
about sex. It's normal to wonder about sex, especially if you
haven't experienced it and everyone seems to think it is so
great. Think about it. If there was a place that some of your
friends had gone that sounded really fun and you had seen
it advertised on TV constantly as being
this great place to visit and there were all
kinds of exciting things to do if you went
to this place, wouldn't you think about it

and want to go there? It is much the same for boys and sex. Most boys are anxious to go there because it's being advertised a lot (by the media and sadly by the way some girls are dressed), and they are enthusiastic about experiencing it.

What I don't want you to think is that every time a guy talks to you he is thinking about having sex with you. That's just not accurate. Guys have more on their minds than just sex. But you also must realize that the guys your age are experiencing extremely high levels of "guy hormones," which kick into gear the idea of sex in the first place.

You, by the way, are also experiencing extremely high levels of "girl hormones" that are kicking into gear the idea that guys and relationships with guys are desirable. (And that, by the way, was the reason for your question.) Why would you even care about what a guy is thinking unless you are interested in guys? All this is normal—this new interest you have in guys and this new interest guys have in you. The trick here is not to let the curiosity and interest lead you to places that are off limits for this time in your life.

Love, Dad

Dear Dad,

It seems like we were closer when I was younger.) used to call me your "little princess" and spend time w me. Now you seem distant and sometimes even uncomfo able around me. Why is that?

—Claire, 15

Dear Claire,

I'm so glad you asked because basically I feel t same way. It was easier to find things in common when y were younger. Games of Old Maid or trips to the park we sure bets to bring a smile to your face. As you have gott older, my desire to spend time with you has not diminishe I sometimes feel like we've lost touch or I'm competing wi your friends. Some of the things we used to do, you no consider "uncool," so I'm often at a loss as to what to sug gest when it comes to spending time with you. For exampl I know you enjoy shopping, but I doubt you would real want to tromp around the mall with good ol' dad. I don take it personally as I know that its perfectly normal to pu away from your parents during this season of your life an

*A*s you have gotten older, my desire to spend time with you has not diminished. I some times feel like we've lost touch or I'm competing with your friends. Some of the things we used to do, you now consider "uncool," so I'm often at a loss as to what to even suggest when it comes to spending time.

WORD OF THE WEEK

The Subject: God ordains certain men to hell on purpose

Isaiah 64:8 - O Lord, thou art our Father; we are the clay; and thou our potter; and we all are the <u>work</u> of thy hand.

    <u>work</u> - Hebrew: Maaseh-an action (good or bad); product; transaction; business

Romans 9:20-23 - Who art thou that repliest against God? Shall the thing formed say to him that formed it, why hast thou made me thus? Hath not the potter the power over the clay of the same lump, to make one vessel unto honour and another unto dishonour -- What if God willing to show his wrath, and to make his power known, endured with much long suffering the vessels of wrath fitted to destruction: And that he might make known the riches of his glory on the vessels of mercy, which he hath afore prepared unto glory."

    <u>fitted</u> - Greek: katartizo - to complete thoroughly; fit; frame; arrange; prepare. Thayer says this word speaks of men whose souls God has so constituted that they cannot escape destruction; <u>their mind is fixed that they frame themselves.</u>

Men get angry to think that we serve a God that can do as it pleases him. They actually think that an almighty God thinks the way they think and that he could not possibly form-fit a vessel to hell merely to show his wrath and power. Paul said he does. Men have difficulty perceiving a God that predestinates men (Rom. 8:29) on whom he desires to show his grace (unmerited favor) and mercy, that he may shower them throughout eternity with the riches of his glory. We like to believe that we must give him permission; if he is to operate in our hearts and minds. The Lord said, "My thoughts are not your thoughts, neither are your ways my ways. As the heavens are higher than the earth, so are my ways higher than your ways and my thoughts than your thoughts (Isaiah 55:8,9)". Our God is in the heavens: he hath done whatsoever he hath pleased (Psalms 115:3). He doeth whatsoever pleaseth him (Eccl 8:3). Thou, O Lord hast done as it pleased thee (Jonah 1:14). Whatsoever the Lord pleased, that did he in heaven, and earth, and in the seas. and in all deep places (Psalms 135:6). He does all his pleasure (Isa. 46:10; Isa. 44:24-28; Eph. 1:5,9; Philippians 2:13). It is Jesus that holds the keys to death and hell (Rev. 1:18), not Satan. God will intentionally cast these evil vessels of wrath into hell and lock them up for eternity because it is not his pleasure to draw them to him (John 6:44). This doctrine angers men, though it is taught throughout the pages of God's Holy Book. Men do not have a Biblical view of the living God when they think he is not in control of all things including the minds and hearts of all men. God is not only love to the vessels of mercy, but he is a consuming fire (Deut 4:24) upon the vessels of wrath fitted to destruction. We do not serve a God who is Superman that can only shake mountains, implode blackholes, and explode quasars. The God of the universe can harden and soften the hearts of men at will (Rom 9:18; Ezek. 36:26). He giveth not account of any of his matters (Job 33:13).

GRACE AND TRUTH MINISTRIES
P.O. Box 1109 Hendersonville, TN 37077
Jim Brown - Bible Teacher - 824-8502

Radio Broadcast – Sat. Morn. 8am 1300 AM Dial WNQM
TV – Mon. & Sat 10pm, Wed. & Fri. 12am Channel 176;
Tues. & Thurs. 5pm Channel 3; Thurs. 11am Channel 49

Join us for fellowship at 394 West Main Street on
Sunday Mornings @ 11:00am, Sunday Evenings @ 7:00pm,
Wednesday Evenings @ 7:00pm
Or
Watch us live via U-Stream on the web at
www.graceandtruth.net

*I*t's a whole different ball game when you have a daughter and all of a sudden the reality hits you that someday this precious little girl is going to grow up into a beautiful young lady that guys will notice.

gravitate more toward your friends. It is part of the process that prepares you to someday leave the nest.

Now that we've both determined that we want to spend time together, I have a suggestion. Think of a few things you would like to do (dads are not real good at guessing games—just ask your mom!). If you feel weird telling me what those things are, try e-mailing them to me and give me some suggested times when you are available. Most importantly, remember that you are never too old to be my "little princess."

Love, Dad

Dear Dad,

Why do dads make such a big deal about dating? I don't get the whole "you have to be blah-blah age before you are allowed to go on a car date" speech. What are dads so afraid of anyway?

—Cassie, 14

Dear Cassie,

What are we afraid of? Where do I begin? For starters, you have to remember that we used to be teenage boys; and even though it may have been a while back, we still remember what teenage boys are capable of when it comes to dating relationships. It's a whole different ball game when you have a daughter, and all of a sudden the reality hits you that someday this precious little girl is going to grow up into a beautiful young lady that guys will notice.

When you were a toddler, I seriously considered praying that your cute little habit of picking your nose would continue well into the teen years in order to

repel the boys. As your father, I am called to protect you; and I admit, sometimes I might go overboard. I am trying hard to learn the balance of when to let go and when to cling tight. It's especially hard to let go when I have these occasional flashbacks of my own teen years. A zillion questions run through my mind. Will they show you respect? Will they drive too fast? Do they drink or do drugs? Will guys pressure you sexually? Will they get you home by curfew?

Someday, when you have kids, you will realize how hard it is for parents to let go of their children. For dads it can be especially hard to let our daughters go. Our motive is not to squelch your social life but rather to love and protect you.

Try to remember that the next time you think we are go[ing] overboard with our dating rules. I will try to work on trusti[ng] God more with my insecurities. In the meantime, if someo[ne] wants to date you, have him contact me. I am happy [to] e-mail him the twenty-two page application I creat[ed] to screen out the weirdos.

Love, Dad

MY FATHER
WHO ART IN HEAVEN

by Whitney Prosp

Father. What comes to mind when you hear that word? Maybe it's wonderful images of sitting on your dad's lap listening to him tell you stories. Or it's when he helped you learn how to ride a bike or pitch a softball. We all have a mental picture that flashes in our mind when we hear the word *father.*

So when we read in the Bible that God is our heavenly Father, we transfer the memories we have of our earthly father to God. For those with a father who nurtured and loved them, it's easy to believe that God will do the same. For those whose dads met their physical and emotional needs, they find it easier to tru God. But what about those who had fathe who didn't love and care for them?

Maybe when you hear that God is yo heavenly Father, it is anything but go news. Your dad wasn't there for you. May he left. Or you never knew him. Or yo wished you had never met him. Or may he was abusive and cruel. Does that me that God is the same way? Will God hurt yo if you trust him? Will he string you alo to make you think you can trust him an then all of a sudden, just when your gua is down, hurt you in some horrible way?

Maybe your dad was there but just never seemed to have enough energy or love to give you. He was basically emotionally absent and had so many problems of his own that he couldn't find love to give you. You wonder if God will treat you in the same way. You're afraid that if you really trust that he'll love you, you'll end up disappointed and betrayed. Again.

If this is you, let's take a look at what the Bible says about your heavenly Father. Romans 8:15 says, "For you did not receive a spirit of slavery to fall back into fear, but you received the Spirit of adoption, by whom we cry out, 'Abba Father!'" Do you know what the word *Abba* means? It means daddy. Even though God holds the entire universe in his hand and is all-powerful and all-knowing, he is still a daddy. He has a daddy's heart. But he's not just any daddy. He's a perfect daddy. He has your best interests in mind at all times. He will care for your needs. He is tender,

your life.

It's one thing to know this in your head, but it's much different to let it sink down into your heart. That may take some time, and that's OK. But if you need God to do a total makeover of how you see him, start by asking him to do so. Simply ask him to change the way you view him. Pray that he will help you realize what images come to mind when you think of the word *dad*, and then evaluate them to see if they fit into the kind of Father he really is. You may find that so many assumptions you made about your heavenly Father are simply not true.

You may even want to start with a list. You could brainstorm the top five characteristics that come

ROMANS 8:15 SAYS, "FOR YOU DID NOT RECEIVE A SPIRIT OF SLAVERY TO FALL BACK INTO FEAR, BUT YOU RECEIVED THE SPIRIT OF ADOPTION, BY WHOM WE CRY OUT, 'ABBA FATHER!'"

compassionate, forgiving and strong. And he is free to love. He, unlike some human fathers, isn't shackled to past pain that keeps him from loving you. He can love you freely and unconditionally, for all of

to your mind when you think of the word *father*. Now take all of those traits and see if they match what he says about himself in the Word. A good place to start is the words of Jesus. Why? Because he said in John 14:9, "The one who has seen Me has seen the Father." So if you want to know what the heavenly Father is like, just look at Jesus. Was Jesus loving? Yes, and so is the Father. Was he forgiving and compassionate? Oh, yes. If you want to know if the traits that come to your mind when you think of father describe the way God really is, just look in the Bible.

You may need to take your old image of father and exchange it with a new one. It's kind of like changing a picture on your wall. Have you ever made your mom take down the one with you in brac sporting a bad haircut and replace it with the ne est you? Well, it's kind of like doing that. You'll wa to take down the picture of "dad" that you've hu on the wall of your mind. It's not that you dor have anything to do with your father anymore, ju that you realize and embrace the fact that you ha another Father who is perfect in every way. Repla that old image with a portrait of your heaven Father.

And remember th isn't a one-time deal. It a process. You may fin that you're constantl taking down old image and replacing them wit new ones. For you it ma take a few months o years, or it even migh take a whole lifetime o reminding yourself wha your Father is like.

No father is perfect Even those friends yo suspect have perfect fami lies have some level of pair and problems. God isn' asking you to forsake you earthly father. He simply calls you to remember that he is a Father who will never let you down. He will always be there when you need him. He is never too busy to listen.

Why don't you take some time today to prac- tice what it means to be a little girl again. Take a few minutes to climb into your Daddy's lap. Find a quiet place where you can be alone and read some passages from his Word

YOU MAY NEED TO TAKE YOUR OLD IMAGE OF FATHER AND EXCHANGE IT WITH A NEW ONE. IT'S KIND OF LIKE CHANGING A PIC- TURE ON YOUR WALL: REPLACE THAT OLD IMAGE WITH A PORTRAIT OF YOUR HEAVENLY FATHER.

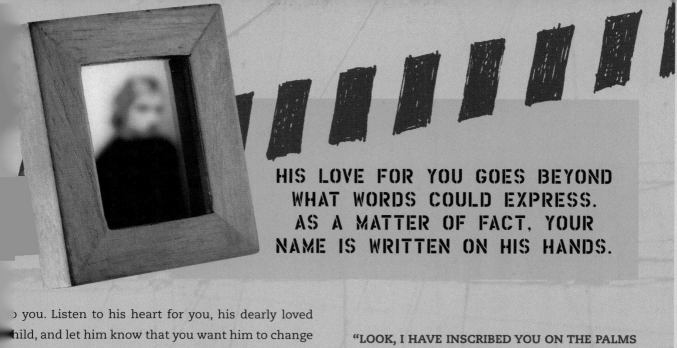

HIS LOVE FOR YOU GOES BEYOND
WHAT WORDS COULD EXPRESS.
AS A MATTER OF FACT, YOUR
NAME IS WRITTEN ON HIS HANDS.

o you. Listen to his heart for you, his dearly loved
hild, and let him know that you want him to change
our view of how you see him. Ask him to help you
rust him as a little girl trusts her loving father.
Remember that he loves you more than you could
ver imagine. His love for you goes beyond what
words could express. As a matter of fact, your name
s written on his hands.

"LOOK, I HAVE INSCRIBED YOU ON THE PALMS
OF MY HANDS; YOUR WALLS ARE CONTINUALLY
BEFORE ME." (ISAIAH 49:16) *

Can You Relate?

1. What picture comes to mind when you
   hear the word *father*?

2. When you think of God as your heavenly Father, how does that make you feel?

3. Describe the kind of Father you think God is.

4. Do you need to ask God to change your perception of father? If so, write
   a short prayer asking him to do just that.

the truth about Charm

by Vicki Courtney

Not long ago my publicist forwarded an e-mail to me she had received from the producer of a radio show. I had done an interview for his show the day before on the subject of Internet safety. The e-mail said, "Vicki was absolutely charming, and we plan to have her on the show again in the future." I have to admit that I smiled when I read the word *charming*. What a great word! Who doesn't want to be referred to as "charming"? The dictionary defines *charm* as the "ability to attract or delight greatly." So how does one obtain the elusive quality of charm? And where exactly, does it fit in our Christian walk? Is charm on God's list of approved qualities?

I have a collection of vintage *Seventeen* magazines and just may have stumbled upon the secret to charm while thumbing through an issue from October 1949. An article by a "noted beauty authority" addressed the three fundamentals of charm. Get ready to laugh.

The three fundamentals of charm are:

Vigorous aliveness

Appealing good looks

Ability to meet life gaily

Get ready to laugh even more. The author goes on to [str]ess the importance of "physical well-being" as the secret [to] the three fundamentals of charm and summed it up by [sa]ying, "You can't be gay [I swear it says this], you can't [be] vigorous, and you can't look your best if you're not in [go]od condition." That advice may have been helpful in 1949, [bu]t I'm thinking it's a bit outdated for the average teen girl [to]day.

So what exactly does God have to say about charm? [D]oes the Bible even address it? Amazingly, it does. Proverbs [31]:30 says, "Charm is deceptive and beauty is fleeting, but [a] woman who fears the LORD will be praised." The original [H]ebrew word for *deceptive* in the verse is *sheqer* and it [m]eans "an untruth" or "a sham." When I think of the word [sh]am, I think of an e-mail I just got this morning from a [fr]iend. It included a touching story and then, at the end,

God speaks of is quite different. It is an awe and reverence for him—an awesome respect. One Bible dictionary describes fear of the Lord as something that:

- dreads God's displeasure
- desires God's favor
- reveres God's holiness
- submits cheerfully to God's will
- is grateful for God's benefits
- sincerely worships God
- conscientiously obeys God's commandments

Proverbs 31:30 says, **"Charm is deceptive and beauty is fleeting, but a woman who fears the LORD will be praised."**

it said that if I didn't forward it to ten friends right away, something bad might happen to me. Hmmm. I deleted the e-mail and discounted it as a sham. A sham is not worth my time. I have more important matters to deal with than going through my address book in an attempt to safeguard my future. Equally, the pursuit of charm is not worth my time. Why invest in something that bids for the attention of man when I should care more about pleasing my heavenly Father?

The second part of Proverbs 31:30 is clear on what makes God's list when it comes to admirable qualities. "A woman who fears the Lord will be praised." So what in the world does it mean to "fear the Lord"? When I hear the word *fear,* I think of knees knocking, teeth chattering, I-just-saw-a-ghost kind of fear. Is God talking about that kind of fear? Does he want us to be afraid of him? The "fear" that

Let's break down the variables above to understand what is involved in fearing the Lord. This is an opportunity for you to do a self-assessment and ask yourself where you stand in regard to each variable.

DO YOU DREAD GOD'S DISPLEASURE? You know that feeling you get when one of your parents is disappointed in you over something you have done? Would it concern you if you knew God was displeased with your actions? Would it motivate you to avoid displeasing him?

DO YOU DESIRE GOD'S FAVOR? Are you more concerned with winning the favor of man or God? Sadly, most Christians seem more concerned with being people-pleasers rather than God-pleasers.

DO YOU REVERE GOD'S HOLINESS? Do you use the name of the Lord in vain or remain silent when others use his name in vain. Or do you cringe when you hear someone blaspheme his holy name? The culture may find it cute to refer to Jesus as a "homeboy," but you know better. Someone who dies for sinners deserves to be called Savior, not "homeboy."

DO YOU SUBMIT CHEERFULLY TO GOD'S WILL? Are you committed to seeking out God's will by reading the Bible consistently and praying? When you know what God wants you to do in a situation, do you do it, even though it may not be the popular thing to do?

ARE YOU GRATEFUL FOR GOD'S BENEFITS? Do you regularly thank him for all he has done for you? Or do you focus more in your prayer time on what you would like him to do for you? Do you face life with an attitude that says the glass is half full rather than half empty? The truth is, with God at the center, it is overflowing.

DO YOU SINCERELY WORSHIP GOD? Do you recogn[ize] that worship is more than a song offered to God in a chu[rch] service? Do you see worship as an attitude of the he[art] that is constantly aware that "God is God, and I'm not."

DO YOU CONSCIENTIOUSLY OBEY GOD'S COMMAN[D]MENTS? Do you filter decisions through God's co[m]mandments set forth in the Bible? Has it become seco[nd]

DO YOU DREAD GOD'S DISPLEASURE?
DO YOU DESIRE GOD'S FAVOR?
DO YOU REVERE GOD'S HOLINESS?
DO YOU SUBMIT CHEERFULLY TO GOD'S WILL?
ARE YOU GRATEFUL FOR GOD'S BENEFITS?
DO YOU SINCERELY WORSHIP GOD?
DO YOU CONSCIENTIOUSLY OBEY GOD'S COMMANDMENTS

ture for you to obey first and ask
estions later?

So how did you do? Don't
at yourself up if you fall short.
member, we are a work in progress
hen it comes to spiritual matu-
y. The truth is, we probably all
ave room for improvement when
comes to fearing the Lord. If you
e struggling to fear him, start by
aying and sharing your struggle
ith God. Ask him to help you focus
our attention on learning what it
eans to fear him. And then work on
he list above by putting your fear
f the Lord into practice.

Remember wise old King Solomon in the
ld Testament? At God's prompting he wrote
he beautiful book of Ecclesiastes. He was best
nown for possessing great wisdom. He had per-
onally reaped the benefits of wealth, knowledge,
nd power, yet he continued to question the
eaning of life throughout his years. At the end
of Ecclesiastes, he concludes with this:

> **"Now all has been heard; here is the conclusion of the matter: Fear God and keep his commandments, for this is the whole duty of man." (Ecclesiastes 12:13 NIV)**

Let me sum it up for you in a nut-
shell: When all is said and done, and
someday you stand before your Maker,
charm will be powerless on the One
that matters most. *

Can You Relate?

1. Has anyone ever called you "charming"? If so, what were the circumstances and how did it make you feel?

2. If the Bible tells us that "charm is deceptive and beauty is fleeting," why do you think so many girls still chase after charm and beauty?

3. When you read over the variables of what it is to "fear the Lord," which ones are you weak in?

4. Overall, would you say that you show a healthy awe and reverence for God?

5. Would others close to you say that you are more focused on beauty and charm or fearing the Lord?

benefits to
Fearing the Lord

by Vicki Courtney

Don't worry, we don't expect you to have the Bible memorized. This quiz is open book! There's no excuse not to make a perfect score, but the real prize is reaping in the benefits that come with fearing the Lord!

1. According to Psalm 34:9, those who fear the Lord, will

a) gain knowledge.

b) lack nothing.

2. According to Psalm 111:10, the fear of the Lord is the

a) end to suffering.

b) beginning of wisdom.

3. According to Psalm 115:13, those who fear the Lord will be

a) blessed.

b) healthy.

4. According to Psalm 128:1, those who fear the Lord are

a) rich.

b) happy.

5. According to Proverbs 10:27, the fear of the Lord

a) prolongs life.

b) brightens your countenance.

6. According to Proverbs 14:27, the fear of the Lord is

a) the secret to great wealth.

b) the fountain of life.

According to Proverbs 15:16, "Better a little with the fear of the LORD than

　　a) many words with empty promises.

　　b) great treasure with turmoil.

According to Proverbs 15:33, the fear of the Lord

　　a) teaches patience.

　　b) teaches wisdom.

According to Proverbs 19:23, the fear of the Lord leads to life and one will

　　a) sleep at night without danger.

　　b) face each day with a smile.

10. According to Isaiah 33:6, the fear of the Lord is the key to

　　a) the cattle on a thousand hills.

　　b) a rich store of salvation, wisdom, and knowledge.

SECRET ANSWERS!

Can You Hear Me Now?

by Whitney Prosperi

What comes to your mind when you think of prayer? Do you picture long robes and hard wooden pews? Or do you flash back to the last time you really tried to give prayer a shot and woke up an hour later after a long snooze on your bed? If you're like most people, prayer is something that doesn't come easily. We often have the best intentions, but it's hard to know where to start and how to stay interested. Let's look at some ways to strengthen our prayer muscles and really begin to enjoy our time praying instead of dreading it.

1

Start small. Take some pressure off yourself. If you go to church, you've probably heard a zillion times that you should pray. It's not that you don't want to; you just find it hard to stay consistent. Try this: instead of deciding to pray for an hour, why not set aside ten minutes? Or if that seems like too much, start with five. It's kind of like working out. The first time you walk or jog that mile, it may seem hard; but the more you "just do it," the easier it gets; and over time you can go longer. After a while, prayer will become a normal part of your routine, like brushing your teeth or doing crunches before bed. It will be something you look forward to and enjoy.

2

Set yourself up for success. Have you ever noticed that as soon as you sit down to pray you remember forty-seven things that you should be doing? I know that my mind whirls with my to-do list and all of the things I never even had time to write on that list. And to make matters worse, it seems that as soon as I sit down to pray the phone rings or something happens to interrupt me. Can you relate? If so, make a plan to eliminate distractions. Why not turn off your cell phone and computer? Find a quiet place where no one will interrupt you. You might even want to put a note on your bedroom door stating your need

a few minutes of privacy. If you share a bedroom, why not head into your closet (assuming there is room in there and you won't be tempted to organize your shoes)? The more you purpose to get alone and quiet, the easier it will be to talk with God.

3 Remember the relationship.
When you were little, did you go see Santa Claus at the mall with your Christmas list each year? I remember the year I took him a picture out of a catalog just in case he needed to know where to find the exact toy I wanted. Well, while God isn't like Santa Claus, in many ways we treat him like he is. We spend our prayer time reciting all of the things he needs to fix, change, and give us. Now it's important to know that God does want to hear our needs. In fact, Isaiah 30:18 says, "Therefore the Lord is waiting to show you mercy, and is rising up to show you compassion, for the LORD is a just God. Happy are all who wait patiently for Him." But it's important to remember that prayer isn't simply firing off our requests; it's spending time with God. Think of all of the times when you've called a friend just to talk. You didn't have a list of things to tell her; you just wanted to hear her voice. When was the last time you prayed just because you wanted to spend some time with God?

4 Change it up. One way to keep things fresh in your relationship with God is to break from the norm every now and then. If you always read from a certain devotional or pray in a certain place, just one simple change may add a new dimension to your time with him. Why not take a prayer walk? You could even talk aloud to him, and if you're concerned with people thinking you've lost it, put your headphones on. They'll think you're singing to the music.

Or find a neat journal and cool pen to record your prayers. Why not type and store your prayers on your computer? Or write a poem or song in response to God's love for you. Another idea is to make a date with God—and then keep it. Just like any other date, you'll want to plan what you'll do and where you'll go. Be as creative as you can. The more thought and effort you put into your time alone with God, the easier it will be to beef up those prayer muscles.

5 Don't spend the whole time talking.
Have you ever had a friend who talked ten times more than she listened? I have, and trust me, it can be exhausting. You probably know the feeling. Just when you want to say something, even if it's that you have to get off the phone, you can't get a word in edgewise.

Sometimes I think that's how God must feel. Now don't get me wrong; he could certainly break in if he wanted to. After all, he made our mouths, and it's by his grace that we can make a peep. But often when we spend time talking with him, that's all we do: talk. And when we do that, we miss out on what God wants to say to us, which is so much more important than what we want to say to God anyway.

The next time you pray, take some time to really listen to him. Just quiet your heart and mouth and ask him to speak o you. He may bring a Bible verse to your mind (Are you tucking Bible verses in your mind for him to remind you of?)

or point out an area of your life that needs a change. Or may just assure you of His love for you. One of the bigg ways he speaks to us today is through his Word. Do you list to his Word each day by reading your Bible? Don't make t mistake of doing all the talking. If you do, you'll miss out the coolest part of prayer. The part where the God that cr ated the whole entire universe talks to you—little, tiny you

Can You Relate?

"Trust in Him at all times, you people; pour out your hearts before Him. God is our refuge."
Psalm 62:8

1. If you had to describe your prayer life in one phrase, what would it be?

2. What can you do to eliminate distractions when you pray?

3. In a typical prayer time do you spend more time telling God what you need or listening to what he has to say? Be honest.

4. What will you do this week to change up your prayer time?

5. How much priority do you give to reading and memorizing God's Word? In what ways will you beef up your daily intake from the Bible?

1. **Never ever** forget you are loved by God.

2. **Never ever** make sin a lifestyle of choice.

3. **Never ever** discard God's free gift of eternal life through Jesus Christ.

4. **Never ever** assume that your sin is too great to be forgiven.

5. **Never ever** think you can outrun God.

6. **Never ever** forget that you are wonderfully made.

7. **Never ever** think that you have to pray with your eyes closed.

8. **Never ever** let your love relationship with God become stale.

9. **Never ever** lose sight of the fact that the Bible is able to change your thinking.

10. **Never ever** let God become second in your life to anyone or anything else.

google a sinner?

By Vicki Courtney

liar

We've all done wrong things. But what if ou
sins were made public for all to see? Believe it or not, some criminals
have experienced a dose of public shame as part of sentence for their
crimes. Consider this:

In Maryland, Texas, Georgia, and California, shoplifters have been
required to stand outside stores with signs announcing their crimes.

In Florida and Ohio, drunken drivers are issued special license plates
that identify them to fellow motorists.

In Houston and Corpus Christi, Texas, convicted sex offenders
have been ordered to place signs on their front lawns that warn
away children.

In Pennsylvania, the driver of a car that caused a fatal accident was
forced to carry a picture of the victim.

In North Carolina, four young offenders who broke into a school and
did $60,000 in damage were ordered to wear signs around their necks
in public that read "I AM A JUVENILE CRIMINAL."

In Ohio, two teens who, on Christmas Eve 2002, had defaced a statue
of Jesus they stole from a church's nativity scene, had to deliver a
new statue to the church and march through town with a donkey and
a sign reading "Sorry for the Jackass Offense."

One can only wonder if the public shame and humiliation deterred these criminals from committing future crimes. Aren't you glad that God doesn't keep a public ledger of our sins? Imagine for a minute what it would be like if you could simply google someone's name and up popped a link that posted a chronological listing of each and every sin the person in question had committed. Google-a-sinner at your fingertips. Date, time, nature of offense—all available for the public's viewing pleasure. And imagine how freaky it would be if it also listed the person's future sins. Imagine how handy the list would be to potential employers, soon-to-wed fiancés, business partners, teachers, parents, and anyone basically looking for revealing information. It might sound appealing if you could google other people's sin lists, but you sure wouldn't want anyone to google yours!

For grins' sake, let's take it a step further. Let's say that next to each sin, there is a rating from one to one hundred, depending on the severity of the offense. At the top, next to the person's name is a number that represents the running total average of all the offenses. Similar to those fancy mattress stores that calculate a person's sleep number, imagine if every person was given a "sin number." Even more humbling is the thought that each day new sins are added to the top of the list. In fact, for many, just refreshing the page every hour would bring up pages of new sins. Every thought, word, or deed committed that is not pleasing to God. Pretty scary, huh?

> Psalm 103:12 says, "As far as the east is from the west, so far has He removed our transgressions from us." In case you are wondering how far it is between the east and the west, the two never meet.

Fortunately, no one has access to our list of sins except for God. And for the Christian, the Bible is clear on what he does with the sins on that list. Psalm 103:12 says, "As far as the east is from the west, so far has He removed our transgressions from us." In case you are wondering how far it is between the east and the west, the two never meet. Holocaust survivor, Corrie Ten Boom, once said that God casts our sins into the deepest ocean and then places a sign in the spot that says, 'No Fishing Allowed.' Unfortunately, a lot of people see God as some kind of angry judge who sits behind a fancy mahogany desk with a gavel in hand just waiting to lower the boom on anyone who misbehaves. Some Christians mistakenly believe that God, like some of the judges in the court cases above who made the guilty parties wear signs displaying their wrongdoings, wants us to carry the burden and shame of our sins.

I'll admit, the whole concept of a loving God who forgets our sins is a bit heavy to take in. When I became a Christian at the age of twenty-one, I had a hard time believing that God really forgot about my sins and no longer held them against me. I mean, I had some real biggies on that sin list, and it just seemed to me that he would want me to suffer punishment. I had already suffered the consequences of many of these sins, but it didn't seem like enough. So I told others about his wonderful offer of forgiveness to those who believe in the name of Jesus, but deep down inside I wasn't sure I believed it for myself.

your sin number is:
78

There were a couple of sins on my sin list that haunted me more than all the others. Even after becoming a Christian, I just couldn't believe that God would really forgive me for these sins. I beat myself up with shame over the years.

> Hebrews 4:16 encourages us to approach God's throne of grace with confidence, so we may receive mercy and find grace to help us in our time of need.

I'm surprised my knees didn't buckle from carrying the weight of these sins. And then one day, while attending a Christian women's event, the speaker shared a verse that I had heard a thousand times before. Something clicked, and God brought that verse to life in my heart. She was sharing about Jesus' death on the cross and reminded us of his final words on the cross. John 19:30 says, "When he had received the drink, Jesus said, 'It is finished.' With that, he bowed his head and gave up his spirit" (NIV). Did you catch that? *It is finished.* Pretty simple statement but loaded with life-changing meaning. As I was sitting there pondering the meaning and magnitude of that verse, it was as if God spoke these words to my heart: "Vicki, it is finished. The price has been paid. I didn't footnote my statement with any sort of conditions like, 'It is finished . . . unless you have had sex outside of marriage,' or 'It is finished . . . unless you have had an

abortion.' I just said, 'It is finished.' I no longer remember these sins. Child, it's time to lay them down." And lay them down, I did. I don't have the luxury of forgetting my sins like God does, but when I remember them, I no longer feel shame. Instead, my shame has been replaced with an overflowing heart of gratitude over what God has done for me.

Hebrews 4:16 encourages us to approach God's throne of grace with confidence, so we may receive mercy and find grace to help us in our time of need. Think of a time you needed grace—maybe you committed a sin so atrocious that you still feel uncomfortable at the thought of it. Now picture yourself approaching God's throne of grace. You have an appointment with the King of kings and Lord of lords. He's waiting for you. You begin to approach the great Almighty. Do you walk? Do you run? Do you hang your head low and drag your feet? Once there, what do you say? Your answers to these questions will shed light on how you view God. Do you see him as an angry judge who can't wait to punish you, or do you see him as a loving Father who is ready and willing to forgive?

forgiven!

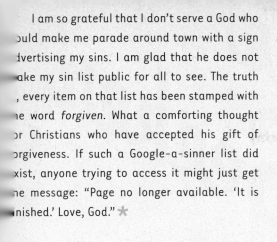

I am so grateful that I don't serve a God who would make me parade around town with a sign advertising my sins. I am glad that he does not make my sin list public for all to see. The truth is, every item on that list has been stamped with the word *forgiven*. What a comforting thought for Christians who have accepted his gift of forgiveness. If such a Google-a-sinner list did exist, anyone trying to access it might just get the message: "Page no longer available. 'It is finished.' Love, God." *

saved by **grace**

Can You Relate?

1. Do you see God as an angry judge or a loving Father?

2. Are you able to approach God's throne with grace and confidence over your sins?

3. If all sins are weighted equally in God's eyes, why do you think we are able to so easily dismiss the "little" sins in our lives? Is this really such a thing as a "little sin"?

4. Consider making a list of your sins on a piece of paper in private. When you are finished, read over it and one at a time, scratch through each sin. Draw a cross over your paper, and at the top put, "It is finished."

5. God's forgiveness is often referred to as the "good news." Why is that? Good news is always worth sharing, right?

Treasure Seeker

by Susie Davis

When I was little, I would beg mom to buy certain cereals the grocery store. It was ually the delicious sug- stuff like Cap'n Crunch Sugar Pops. My mom rely purchased that type cereal because she knew at what I was really after as the toy advertised on the ont of the box. On the occa- ons when she did buy the cereal was begging for, the minute I got ome I would sink my hand deep into the ugary mess, my fingers searching for the rize. As I pushed my little fingers down farther nd farther rustling through the cereal, frantic to ind the toy, cereal would always spill out over the top. With my arm engulfed in the box, I would smile with satis- action when I could finally feel the edges of the bag that held he prize I was after. Slowly, I would pull the toy up through the backaged cereal that continued to spill out all around me. By the time I was finished, the cereal was half gone, and I was a mess. There were even times when I would search and search, unable to find the prize, and resort to dumping the entire con- tents of the cereal box in a big bowl just so I could find it. Then I would carefully try to pour the cereal back in the bag, happy to have found the prize. Eventually my mom (frustrated by the waste I created looking for the treasure in the box) would make

movie plot, the Bible speaks about treasure—the kind that is over- flowing with silver and gold, unspeak- able riches. Did you know that God regards his very Word, the Bible, as treasure itself?

Psalm 119:72 states, "Instruction from Your lips is better for me than thousands of gold and silver pieces." In other words, instruction from God in the Bible is highly valuable. In addition, the Bible is effective. Hebrews 4:12 tells us, "For the word of God is living and effective and

> "For the word of God is living and effective and sharper than any two-edged sword, penetrating as far as to divide soul, spirit, joints, and marrow; it is a judge of the ideas and thoughts of the heart."
>
> Hebrews 4:12

me wait until the cereal was used up the regular way, with peo- ple eating it for breakfast. That was always the worst. And you can be sure that I was eating tons of that stuff just to get the level of the cereal down so I could spot the prize and pull it out. I would do *anything* to get that *treasure*.

There is nothing more fascinating than treasure. Though it seems better suited to days gone by or the latest fictional

sharper than any two-edged sword, penetrating as far as to divide soul, spirit, joints, and marrow; it is a judge of the ideas and thoughts of the heart." This verse provides understanding for what the treasure of God's Word can do for our lives. And yet sometimes we have trouble finding the motivation to read the Bible. I know that I sometimes struggle. Maybe I feel tired. Sometimes

See, the first thing you need to do is believe that God's Word is a treasure that can change your life. The promise on the package is backed by the power of God himself.

I am just really busy. Or sometimes I forget. Then there are times when I try hard to make daily Bible reading a priority, and I carve out some time and sit down with the Bible. Then when I read it, it just seems boring.

What happens when we want to believe that the Bible is all that it says it is; and yet, when we go to read it, we feel that we come up empty-handed? We know the treasure is in there because God promises that it is, but we're just having difficulty finding it.

It's like what happened with me when I was little and I saw that cereal box. I could see the promise on the package, and I knew that I wanted the treasure inside. So the first thing I needed to do was convince my mom to buy the cereal. I needed to get that box home so I could tear into it. After that I had some work to do. I would stick my hand down into it and search around. Sometimes that could be messy and frustrating, but I believed that the promised prize was inside, so I kept after it. I would

search and search, fingers feeling around in the package contents spilling over the top. And then finally there we the times that I just had to eat that cereal every single d to get to the treasure.

See, the first thing you need to do is believe that God Word is a treasure that can change your life. The promis on the package is backed by the power of God himself. he says his Word is living and active and able, then it i If he promises his Word is better than gold, we can count o it being better than gold in our lives.

After buying into the promise, you nee to realize that it is going to take some dig ging around. You might need to try differ ent books of the Bible and see what speak to you at this time in your life. If you are into stories of intrigue and wonder, try reading Genesis and Exodus. If you like practi-cal advice, try Proverbs. If you love poetry or long to feel understood, try Psalms. Perhaps you want to know more about practical daily living: read Galatians, Ephesians, or Philippians. Want to know what happens at the end of all time? Read Revelation. And if you want to know more about Jesus and his life and ministry, read Matthew, Mark, Luke, or John. There is really something for everyone.

And although I didn't much like the way my mom would eventually make me just eat the cereal to get the prize in the cereal box, I have to advise you that it's also the best way to get the treasure of God's Word into your life—reading portions of the Bible day by day. Ingesting the Word of God and getting that treasure inside your soul happens when you are willing to eat a little at a time, every day.

Psalm 34:8 encourages us to "taste and see that the LORD is good." And if you want to see what God can do in your life, be willing to "taste" the Bible every day, and you will begin to get at the treasure deep inside the pages.

So jump in and be a treasure seeker!

Can You Relate?

Do you have a Bible that you can easily understand? If not, see if you can go to the bookstore and get a read-able translation. (*The Every Day with Jesus Bible,* Holman CSB is a great Bible to start with because it has all the Bible sectioned off into easily readable days. It will enable you to read through the entire Bible in one year. Check out this link: www.broadmanholman.com.)

What is the best time in your day for you to read the Bible? Write it down and consider it your appointment with God.

If you feel you are getting dry in your Bible reading time, consider including a book like *My Utmost for His Highest* (teen version) by Oswald Chambers. It is biblically based and will encourage and challenge you.

If you are stalled out with your Bible reading, talk to a couple of your Christian friends and see how they stay fresh spiritually. Maybe even see if you can start encouraging one another by finding short encouraging verses and texting them to one another. Or conference call one another once a week and see who can come up with the greatest "treasure" of the week.

If you want to know more about the Bible, consider going to a study at a local church or joining a club like Fellowship of Christian Athletes or Young Life where you know they are teaching the Bible.

The main part of being a treasure seeker of God's Word is to realize that to get the most reward, you will need to take part in that activity for the rest of your life. Now while that can seem daunting, you can do it. Just like you know you will brush you teeth for the rest of your life or wash your hair for the rest of your life, you can commit to reading the Bible for the rest of your life. Just take it one day at a time. What stands in your way of making that commitment?

Pray this if you'd like to commit to reading your Bible for the rest of your life:

Dear God,
You know my heart. You know that the Bible sometimes overwhelms me, but I know that Your Word is a treasure I want in my life. I desire knowing You and realize You are revealed in the pages of the Bible. Please God, help me to read Your Word daily. Let me fall in love with Your wisdom. Encourage me to read and love the Bible. And God, when I miss a day, help me to know that You aren't angry with me. And don't let me suffer under false guilt either. Instead, just let it motivate me to pick up where I left off. Thank you for the Bible. Thank you for caring about me and my life. Thank you for loving me. Amen.

too busy for God?

It seems that everyone in our culture wants to have lots going on. Maybe we use busyness to help us know we're valued, or maybe it's just the by-product of too many

Have you ever noticed that it's cool to have a lot going on? I mean, when someone asks you what you've been doing, you don't want to say you've been watching the weather channel trying to understand barometric pressure or learning how to tweeze your eyebrows. You want to have something to say. Everyone in our culture seems to want to have lots going

on. Maybe we use busyness to help us know we're valued, or maybe it's just the by-product of too many options. It's just hard to say no when there are so many wonderful things to say yes to.

Whatever the case may be, if we're too busy for God, we're just too busy. Period. If you find yourself in this situation, read on. You'll find some helpful ways to make time for God in spite of a busy day or a busy life.

Make time with God a priority.

You've probably heard it said that we find time for what [we] really care about. You probably take the time to brush [yo]ur hair and get ready each morning. Most likely you give [so]me attention to responding to important calls or e-mails. [An]d you don't miss out on important conversations with [tha]t someone special when he calls or stops by. So why is it [tha]t time with God is often the last thing on our list? We do [i]f we find extra time, but when other things come up, it's [so]metimes the first thing to go.

Could it be that we know God will forgive us? I mean, [i]t's his specialty, right? And we can't always be assured our [tea]cher will forgive us if we're late or that a friend will over[loo]k an unreturned call. So we take advantage of his forgive[ne]ss, knowing that he'll be waiting for us the next time.

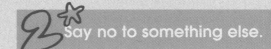

Say no to something else.

While it's not popular to say no to opportunities that come up, sometimes we just have to if we're going to make time with God a top priority. Maybe you're involved in something that takes so much of your time that you're unable to keep your commitment to spend time alone with God. It could be a particular extracurricular activity or interest. If this is the case, consider cutting back time spent on this activity. Or you might even want to take a break from it altogether. You can always get involved in that activity later. The world won't end. I promise. And you might even find that you enjoy having a little free time where you can explore other interests.

[op]tions. It's just hard to say no when there are so many wonderful things to say yes to. [W]hatever the case may be, if we're too busy for God, we're just too busy. Period.

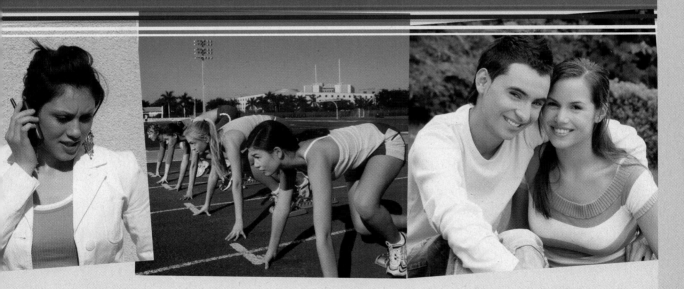

But why not just set time with God as our top priority. [Th]at way other things may not get done or other people may [no]t hear back from us, but God will. We just determine that [ti]me with him is the last thing we toss out on a busy day. If [yo]u're willing to make that commitment, stop right now and [pr]ay. Ask him to help you commit to spending time with him [ea]ch day, whether it is first thing in the morning, right after [sc]hool, or before bed.

Or maybe you are involved in a relationship that takes so much of your time that it's hard for you to squeeze in time with God. Here's a radical thought. Why not turn down the intensity of your relationship? If the other person doesn't understand, then that reveals a lot about him or her. Maybe you don't need to be pouring all of the time into that relationship anyway.

When I was in high school, a friend of mine decided that she was going to give up dating for a season so that she could focus more on her relationship with God. You may not want to do this, or you may be thinking you wish you had a dating life to take a break from, but there may be something else you want to eliminate so you can spend more time with God. It could be time spent on the computer, watching TV, or shopping. Saying no to something else will mean that you can say yes to the very best of all—Jesus.

Maybe you remember the story of Mary and Martha in the Bible. Martha was very busy. She would have fit in beau-

Which person do you identify with more? Will you cho the many things that really don't make a difference or one thing that is absolutely critical? Make the right ch like Mary — and you won't regret it. Ever.

Schedule time with God.

If you're going to stay consistent in spending time God, you have got to set aside the time each day to do Make an appointment with God. It might be in the mor or the evening. It could be during lunch or right after sch

There may be something you want to eliminate so you can sper more time with God. It could be time spent on the compute

tifully in our world. But Mary chose to spend time with Jesus. She knew what was most important. She remembered what would matter in the course of forever. Jesus corrected Martha for the way she chose to live her life and praised Mary for her choices. LUKE 10:41–42 SAYS, "THE LORD ANSWERED HER, 'MARTHA, MARTHA, YOU ARE WORRIED AND UPSET ABOUT MANY THINGS, BUT ONE THING IS NECESSARY. MARY HAS MADE THE RIGHT CHOICE, AND IT WILL NOT BE TAKEN AWAY FROM HER."

What works best for you? For many the morning is the best time to spend time w God. Before the day begins with all of its distractions temptations you can focus on his Word and his perspective

But what if you're not a morning person? That's OK. You'll just have to plan so you can make it up in the morning. You'll want to set your alarm earlier and maybe even have some loud tunes pumping. Do whatever you can to wake up, whether that means a cool shower or a tall glass of ... Getting up to spend time with God is simply a habit that you can work into your day like taking a shower or brushing your teeth. You wouldn't leave the house without combing your hair because it's become a part of your morning ritual. The more mornings you spend with God, the more this will be an irreplaceable step to your morning as well.

Ask a friend for help.

Have you ever noticed that we have an easier time keeping our commitment when we know someone else has made the same one? I used to workout with a friend every morning at six. Now you can bet I wouldn't have dragged myself out of bed if I didn't know she was waiting for me. Having this friend to hold me accountable helped me keep my commitment to getting in shape.

It's the same way in our relationship with God. If you know you want to get up each morning for time alone with

watching TV, or shopping. Saying no to something else will mean that you can say yes to the very best of all—Jesus.

PSALM 143:8 SAYS, "LET ME EXPERIENCE YOUR FAITHFUL LOVE IN THE MORNING, FOR I TRUST IN YOU. REVEAL TO ME THE WAY I SHOULD GO, BECAUSE I LONG FOR YOU."

God but also know you could qualify as an Olympic medallist in pushing the snooze bar, ask a friend to help you. Now I don't mean that she comes to your house and kicks you out of bed. Just agree together to pray for the other one. And then ask each other how you are doing. You may even want to make a deal together. When each of you has consistently gotten up to spend time with God for a week, you could treat each other to ice cream or some other fun treat. Over time you'll understand that the real reward is getting to know more of God, but it doesn't hurt to build in a little incentive when you hold each other accountable.

5 Don't be hard on yourself.

If you miss one day, don't throw in the towel. Just pick up the next day where you left off. Or find a few minutes later in the day to touch base with him. He isn't going to be mad or punish you. He's not asking you to have every little box checked off perfectly. He wants you to get to know h... Remember that this is a relationship. He is waiting to he... from you. ISAIAH 30:18 SAYS, "THEREFORE THE LORD IS WA... ING TO SHOW YOU MERCY, AND IS RISING UP TO SHOW Y... COMPASSION, FOR THE LORD IS A JUST GOD. HAPPY ARE A... WHO WAIT PATIENTLY FOR HIM." ✱

"Therefore the LORD is waiting to show you mercy, and is rising up to show you compassion for the LORD is a just God. Happy are all who wait patiently for Him." Isaiah 30:18

Can You Relate?

1. Is spending time with God each day a priority in your life? Explain your response.

2. Is there an activity or a relationship that you need to step back from in order to have more time with God? If so, how are you going to take the first steps in doing this?

3. What do you think would be the best time for you to spend with God? What will you do to make sure you keep your date with God?

4. Do you have a friend that you could ask to hold you accountable regarding your time spent with God? If so, write her name here. If not, take this time to ask God to bring you such a friend.

5. Are you willing to give up the "much" in order to choose the best thing, time with Jesus? If so, write a prayer asking for his help here.

We Asked...You Told:
your comments about
Spending Time with GOD

survey question: **How do you spend time with God?**

My goal is to have quiet times every morning, but I'll admit that doesn't always happen for me. I think it's a good idea to have daily time with God because it makes my whole day a little better and it helps me grow. —Jana, 15

Every night as I'm lying in bed, I tell God about my day and thank him for all of my blessings. In the morning before school starts, I read the Bible and pray that God would help me be a light in a dark world.
—Deborah, 14

I pull out my guitar and sing my heart out to him. I also bring out my Bible and ask God to show me what he wants me to see that particular night. I seriously open to any page, and it is usually exactly what I need. —Kaylee, 15

I meditate and think about the day. If something comes up and I did something wrong or bad, I ask God for forgiveness and help with all my problems. —Heaven, 15

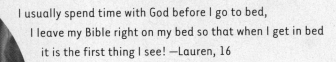

I usually spend time with God before I go to bed, I leave my Bible right on my bed so that when I get in bed it is the first thing I see! —Lauren, 16

Last year I read the *One Year Bible*. It was good because it took about 15 minutes each day and it gives you a psalm, a proverb, and an Old and New Testament passage. Sometimes it's hard to keep up with, though. —Taylor, 15

Right now I'm reading a chapter out of Galatians each week along with some other girls in my D-group at church. —Kelli, 13

I try to do devotions and read the Bible as much as I can. I pray a lot during the day at school, and it helps me have a better day! —Mackenzie, 13

I read a daily devotional. I spend time with God while listening to my Christian music and learning to do sign language to the words. —Kaitlyn, 13

I'm super busy with school and sports, so its hard to find time to relax and spend quality time with God. I found that since I'm a morning person, its best for me to wake up 20 minutes early, before I need to get ready for school, to do my devotion book. —Rosemary, 14

I write my prayers in a journal, and it helps me to pour out my feelings and thoughts to him. I also write down verses out of the Bible that I want to memorize or remember. —Nicole, 15

I always try to take time every day, whether it is reading the Bible, a devotional book, or just listening and worshipping along with Christian music. —Stephanie, 17

I used to push God to the side and wait to spend time with him until Sundays. But now I've realized that is not what he wants. Instead of spending 30 minutes in the morning doing my makeup or hair, I take 5 to 10 minutes of that time to talk with God. At first I didn't know how I would turn out looking if I didn't spend all this time on making myself look pretty, but it has made me feel better about myself by starting every day talking to God. —Jaime, 14

I spend time at night reading my Bible. I have a one-minute-a-day study Bible that I read every day, and I usually read a chapter or two in my Bible. —Lauren, 15

I read my Bible every night, right before I go to bed. I usually read one chapter, and I write down my thoughts in a notebook about what I'm reading. After I do that, I try to write a prayer to God. I like writing out my prayers because it helps me stay focused. My mind isn't drifting off to a million random things at once! Plus it helps me get my thoughts and feelings out too. —Brittany, 15

I try to set aside a time with no distractions to do a small Bible reading/devotion, but sometimes I have a quiet time when I'm driving on my way to school. I pray and sing along with praise music. Sometimes I find a Christian speaker on the radio and listen to that. —Kendra, 16

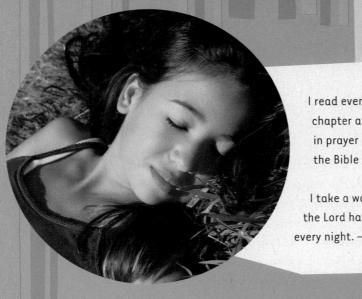

I read every night before I go to bed and I usually read a chapter a day and sometimes journal! I also spend time in prayer every day, and I highlight or underline verses in the Bible that stick out to me. —Kirstie, 14

I take a walk and just open my mind and my heart to what the Lord has to say. I also read my Bible before I go to bed every night. —Dayla, 18

For me, spending time with God is all about just chatting with him before I go to bed. I spend time in prayer, tell him about my day, my feelings, how he has affected me.
—Sarah, 14

Every Friday our family gets together and studies the Bible, which helps me grow closer to God. —Marissa, 15

I try to do it at night right before I go to bed. Sometimes, I'll do it during the moment of silence at school. That may not work for some kids though, because there can be a lot of distractions. —Grace, 12 *

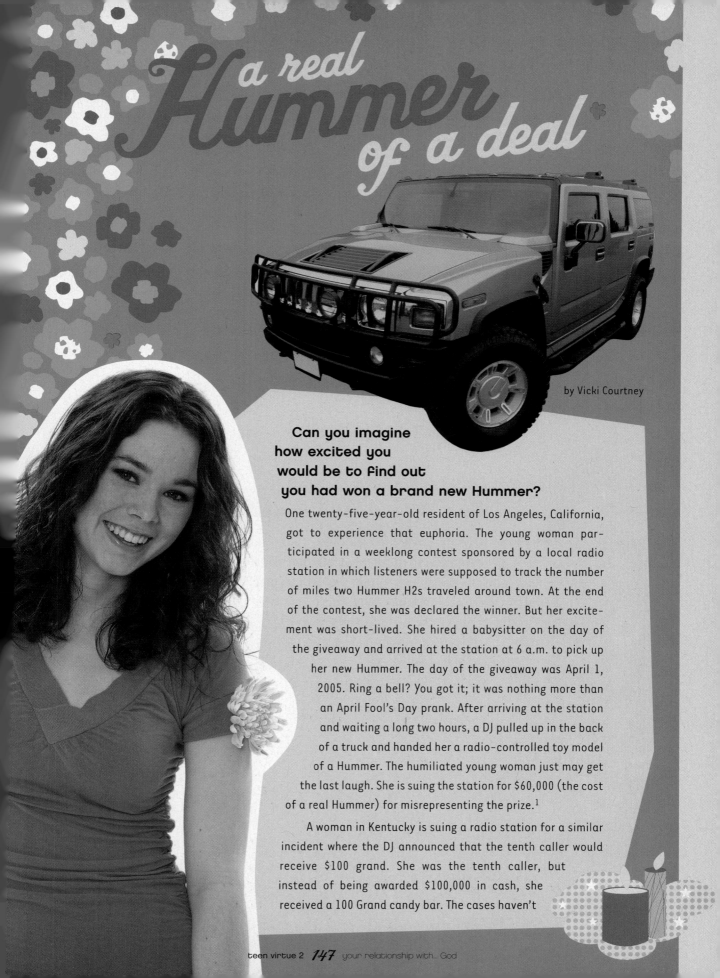

a real Hummer of a deal

by Vicki Courtney

Can you imagine how excited you would be to find out you had won a brand new Hummer?

One twenty-five-year-old resident of Los Angeles, California, got to experience that euphoria. The young woman participated in a weeklong contest sponsored by a local radio station in which listeners were supposed to track the number of miles two Hummer H2s traveled around town. At the end of the contest, she was declared the winner. But her excitement was short-lived. She hired a babysitter on the day of the giveaway and arrived at the station at 6 a.m. to pick up her new Hummer. The day of the giveaway was April 1, 2005. Ring a bell? You got it; it was nothing more than an April Fool's Day prank. After arriving at the station and waiting a long two hours, a DJ pulled up in the back of a truck and handed her a radio-controlled toy model of a Hummer. The humiliated young woman just may get the last laugh. She is suing the station for $60,000 (the cost of a real Hummer) for misrepresenting the prize.[1]

A woman in Kentucky is suing a radio station for a similar incident where the DJ announced that the tenth caller would receive $100 grand. She was the tenth caller, but instead of being awarded $100,000 in cash, she received a 100 Grand candy bar. The cases haven't been settled, but in a similar case involving an April Fool's prank, the pranksters had to pay up. A waitress at a Hooters restaurant in Florida won a contest sponsored by the restaurant where the waitresses were told that the waitress selling the most beer over a one-month period would receive a Toyota. At the end of the month, she was declared the winner, blindfolded, and led out to the parking lot to claim her prize. Unfortunately, when the blindfold was removed, there was no car. In its place was a giant "toy Yoda" Star Wars doll. She sued and won her case. The amount of her winnings was not disclosed, but her lawyer claimed it was enough to "pick out whatever type of Toyota she wants."[2]

Upon hearing the gospel message, many might wonder if it's the real deal. You've probably heard the saying, "If it sounds too good to be true, it probably is." Or maybe, you've heard the one that says, "Nothing in life is ever free." Well, extending the offer of forgiveness to mankind certainly wasn't free to God. He sent his one and only Son, Jesus Christ, to die on the cross for the sins of all people. The cost was great, but all those who believe in Jesus Christ receive forgiveness and eternal life, free of charge. In other words, God doesn't hold the penalty for our sins against us. Sound too good to be true? If you ask me, it's an offer you just can't refuse. Before you claim your prize, check out the print on the next three pages.

---

1. Foxnews.com Out There, 16 July 2005; "Bummer of a Hummer," LOS ANGELES (AP).

2. See www.snopes.com/business/deals/hummer.asp (Hummer Bummer).

God's Love Is Revealed in the Bible

"FOR GOD SO LOVED THE WORLD THAT HE GAVE HIS ONE AND ONLY SON, THAT WHOEVER BELIEVES IN HIM SHALL NOT PERISH BUT HAVE ETERNAL LIFE."
—JOHN 3:16 NIV

God loves you. He wants to bless your life and make it full and complete. And he wants to give you a life that will last forever, even after you experience physical death.

We Are Sinful

**"FOR ALL HAVE SINNED AND FALL
SHORT OF THE GLORY OF GOD."**
—ROMANS 3:23 NIV

You may have heard someone say, "I'm only human—nobody's perfect." This Bible verse says the same thing: We are all sinners. We all do things that we know are wrong. And that's why we feel estranged from God—because God is holy and good, and we are not.

Sin Has a Penalty

"FOR THE WAGES OF SIN IS DEATH."
—ROMANS 6:23 NIV

Just as criminals must pay the penalty for their crimes, sinners must pay the penalty for their sins. If you continue to sin, you will pay the penalty of spiritual death. You will not only die physically; you will also be separated from our holy God for all eternity. The Bible teaches that those who choose to remain separated from God will spend eternity in a place called hell.

Christ Has Paid Our Penalty!

**"BUT GOD DEMONSTRATES HIS OWN LOVE FOR US IN THIS:
WHILE WE WERE STILL SINNERS, CHRIST DIED FOR US."**
—ROMANS 5:8 NIV

The Bible teaches that Jesus Christ, the sinless Son of God, has paid the penalty for all your sins. You may think you have to lead a good life and do good deeds before God will love you. But the Bible says that Christ loved you enough to die for you, even when you were rebelling against him.

Salvation Is a Free Gift

**"FOR IT IS BY GRACE YOU HAVE BEEN SAVED, THROUGH FAITH—AND THIS NOT FROM YOURSELVES,
IT IS THE GIFT OF GOD—NOT BY WORKS, SO THAT NO ONE CAN BOAST."**
—EPHESIANS 2:8–9 NIV

The word *grace* means "undeserved favor." It means God is offering you something you could never provide for yourself: forgiveness of sins and eternal life. God's gift to you is free. You do not have to work for a gift. All you have to do is joyfully receive it. Believe with all your heart that Jesus Christ died for you!

Christ Is at Your Heart's Door

"HERE I AM! I STAND AT THE DOOR AND KNOCK. IF ANYONE HEARS MY VOICE AND OPENS THE DOOR, I WILL COME IN AND EAT WITH HIM, AND HE WITH ME."

—REVELATION 3:20 NIV

Jesus Christ wants to have a personal relationship with you. Picture, if you will, Jesus Christ standing at the door of your heart (the door of your emotions, intellect, and will). Invite him in; he is waiting for you to receive him into your heart and life.

You Must Receive Him

"YET TO ALL WHO RECEIVED HIM, TO THOSE WHO BELIEVED IN HIS NAME, HE GAVE THE RIGHT TO BECOME CHILDREN OF GOD."

—JOHN 1:12 NIV

When you receive Christ into your heart, you become a child of God and have the privilege of talking to him in prayer at any time about anything. The Christian life is a personal relationship to God through Jesus Christ. And best of all, it is a relationship that will last for all eternity.

THEREFORE, IF ANYONE IS IN CHRIST, HE IS A NEW CREATION; THE OLD HAS GONE, THE NEW HAS COME! (2 Corinthians 5:17)

Where do you stand when it comes to God's offer of forgiveness? Have you claimed your grand prize? You can't afford not to—it's a real hummer of a deal.✳

From "Your Christian Life" 1965, 1968, as "Aids to Christian Living," 1986 as "Practical Steps in Christian Living," 1995 as "Beginning Your Christian Life," 1997 as "Your Christian Life," Billy Graham Evangelistic Association.

Can You Relate?

1. Have you claimed your grand prize?

2. What is involved in claiming the prize?

3. What is the payoff to this prize?

4. In your opinion, why do you think some people refuse to receive God's offer of forgiveness (the grand prize)?

5. When was the last time you told someone about this wonderful prize?